A TOPICAL
LOOK AT
THE BOOK
OF PSALMS

A TOPICAL
LOOK AT
THE BOOK
OF PSALMS

Compiled by Eugene Carvalho

A Topical Look at the Book of Psalms

Copyright © 2010 by Eugene Carvalho

In the U.S. write:
Eugene Carvalho
500 Waterman Avenue
East Providence, RI 02914
Telephone: 401 215 3171
Facsimile: 401 438 1992
Web Site: www.newwinemissions.info

ISBN 10: 1461054656
ISBN 13: 978-1461054658

Printed in the United States of America

To my fiancée
Mercedes Serna Chávez.
Thank you for all your love, support
and prayers. With love…

TABLE OF CONTENTS

PURPOSE & ACKNOWLEDGEMENTS

The infallible Word of God for faith and conduct informs us that the Holy Spirit gives gifts to men and women of the Body of Christ. It states: "the gifts edify the body for the building up of the saints" (Eph. 4:12). I hope the talents and gifts the Lord has given me will be a blessing to someone else through the reading of this compilation.

I am grateful for the love from all family members, especially my parents Mary and Eugenio Carvalho. I am also grateful for the knowledge, wisdom and love of many pastors, teachers, and saints that the Lord has used to bless me. Lastly, I must not forget a special thank you to my dear friend Kathryn Regan for proofreading this material.

LAYING A FOUNDATION

I must start off by giving the Lord a shout of praise for using me to write another Christian book for His glory. The Lord put the desire in my heart to write this book about three years ago and I am grateful to be working on it now. It is vital to understand clearly that a Christian must base everything they believe and lay a foundation solely on what is written in the Bible.

Our minds must be renewed day by day by God's precious Word. I want to introduce three sets of Scriptures that will reinforce our vital need to study the Scriptures on a daily basis. The Bible says, "So faith comes from hearing, and hearing by the word of Christ" (Ro. 10:17).[1] "This book of the law shall not depart from your mouth, but you shall meditate on it day and night, so that you may be careful to do according to all that is written in it; for then you will make your way prosperous, and then you will have success" (Jos. 1:8). "...If you continue in My word, then you are truly disciples of Mine; and you will know the truth, and the truth will make you free" (Jn. 8:31-32).

This is why I consider it an honor to write on a subject matter that will bless others for the glory of God. "The book of Psalms is a collection of prayers, poems, and hymns that focus the worshiper's thoughts on God in praise and adoration."[2] The Psalms is perhaps the most widely used section of the entire Bible. They search the full range of human experience in a personal and practical

---

[1] From this point forward all Scripture quotations, unless otherwise noted, are from the *New American Standard Bible*.
[2] Ronald F. Youngblood, *Nelson's New Illustrated Bible Dictionary* (Nashville: Thomas Nelson Publishers, 1995), 1044.

method. Studying the Psalms will strengthen a Christian's Spirit tremendously and bless them to be a blessing to others.

Allow me at this time to mention three more sets of scriptures that inform us of the importance of studying God infallible Word. The Bible says, "Be diligent to present yourself approved to God as a workman who does not need to be ashamed, accurately handling the word of truth" (2 Tim. 2:15). "All Scripture is inspired by God and profitable for teaching, for reproof, for correction, for training in righteousness; so that the man of God may be adequate, equipped for every good work" (2 Tim. 3:16-17). "Preach the word; be ready in season and out of season; reprove, rebuke, exhort, with great patience and instruction" (2 Tim. 4:2).

I suggest you let the Holy Spirit put these scriptures deep inside your Spirit. Do not rush. Each day take one topic and meditate on all of those scriptures. Also, I added a topic index in the back of the book for your convenience.

Chapter Two

A TOPICAL LOOK

ALWAYS
Ps. 9:18 - For the needy will not always be forgotten, Nor the hope of the afflicted perish forever.
Ps. 73:12 - Behold, these are the wicked; And always at ease, they have increased in wealth.
Ps. 103:9 - He will not always strive with us, Nor will He keep His anger forever.

AFRAID
Ps. 3:6 - I will not be afraid of ten thousands of people Who have set themselves against me round about.
Ps. 49:16 - Do not be afraid when a man becomes rich, When the glory of his house is increased.
Ps. 56:3 - When I am afraid, I will put my trust in You.
Ps. 56:4 - In God, whose word I praise, In God I have put my trust; I shall not be afraid. What can mere man do to me?
Ps. 56:11 - In God I have put my trust, I shall not be afraid. What can man do to me?
Ps. 91:5 - You will not be afraid of the terror by night, Or of the arrow that flies by day.
Ps. 119:120 - My flesh trembles for fear of You, And I am afraid of Your judgments.

ANGEL
Ps. 34:7 - The angel of the Lord encamps around those who fear Him, And rescues them.
Ps. 35:5 - Let them be like chaff before the wind, With the angel of the Lord driving them on.

Ps. 35:6 - Let their way be dark and slippery, With the angel of the Lord pursuing them.

ANOINTED

Ps. 2:2 - The kings of the earth take their stand And the rulers take counsel together Against the Lord and against His Anointed.

Ps. 18:50 - He gives great deliverance to His king, And shows lovingkindness to His anointed, To David and his descendants forever.

Ps. 20:6 - Now I know that the Lord saves His anointed; He will answer him from His holy heaven With the saving strength of His right hand.

Ps. 23:5 - You prepare a table before me in the presence of my enemies; You have anointed my head with oil; My cup overflows.

Ps. 28:8 - The Lord is their strength, And He is a saving defense to His anointed.

Ps. 45:7 - You have loved righteousness and hated wickedness; Therefore God, Your God, has anointed You With the oil of joy above Your fellows.

Ps. 84:9 - Behold our shield, O God, And look upon the face of Your anointed.

Ps. 89:20 - I have found David My servant; With My holy oil I have anointed him.

Ps. 89:38 - But You have cast off and rejected, You have been full of wrath against Your anointed.

Ps. 89:51 - With which Your enemies have reproached, O Lord, With which they have reproached the footsteps of Your anointed.

Ps. 92:10 - But You have exalted my horn like that of the wild ox; I have been anointed with fresh oil.

Ps. 105:15 - Do not touch My anointed ones, And do My prophets no harm.

Ps. 132:10 - For the sake of David Your servant, Do not turn away the face of Your anointed.

Ps. 132:17 - There I will cause the horn of David to spring forth; I have prepared a lamp for Mine anointed.

ARISE

Ps. 3:7 - Arise, O Lord; save me, O my God! For You have smitten all my enemies on the cheek; You have shattered the teeth of the wicked.

Ps. 7:6 - Arise, O Lord, in Your anger; Lift up Yourself against the rage of my adversaries, And arouse Yourself for me; You have appointed judgment.

Ps. 9:19 - Arise, O Lord, do not let man prevail; Let the nations be judged before You.

Ps. 10:12 - Arise, O Lord; O God, lift up Your hand. Do not forget the afflicted.

Ps. 12:5 – "Because of the devastation of the afflicted, because of the groaning of the needy, Now I will arise," says the Lord; "I will set him in the safety for which he longs."

Ps. 17:13 - Arise, O Lord, confront him, bring him low; Deliver my soul from the wicked with Your sword.

Ps. 27:3 - Though a host encamp against me, My heart will not fear; Though war arise against me, In spite of this I shall be confident.

Ps. 68:1 - A Song. Let God arise, let His enemies be scattered, And let those who hate Him flee before Him.

Ps. 74:22 - Arise, O God, and plead Your own cause; Remember how the foolish man reproaches You all day long.

Ps. 78:6 - That the generation to come might know, even the children yet to be born, That they may arise and tell them to their children.

Chapter Two

Ps. 82:8 - Arise, O God, judge the earth! For it is You who possesses all the nations.

Ps. 102:13 - You will arise and have compassion on Zion; For it is time to be gracious to her, For the appointed time has come.

Ps. 109:28 - Let them curse, but You bless; When they arise, they shall be ashamed, But Your servant shall be glad.

Ps. 132:8 - Arise, O Lord, to Your resting place, You and the ark of Your strength.

AWE

Ps. 22:23 - You who fear the Lord, praise Him; All you descendants of Jacob, glorify Him, And stand in awe of Him, all you descendants of Israel.

Ps. 33:8 - Let all the earth fear the Lord; Let all the inhabitants of the world stand in awe of Him.

Ps. 65:8 - They who dwell in the ends of the earth stand in awe of Your signs; You make the dawn and the sunset shout for joy.

Ps. 119:161 - Princes persecute me without cause, But my heart stands in awe of Your words.

AWESOME

Ps. 45:4 - And in Your majesty ride on victoriously, For the cause of truth and meekness and righteousness; Let Your right hand teach You awesome things.

Ps. 65:5 - By awesome deeds You answer us in righteousness, O God of our salvation, You who are the trust of all the ends of the earth and of the farthest sea.

Ps. 66:3 - Say to God, "How awesome are Your works! Because of the greatness of Your power Your enemies will give feigned obedience to You."

Ps. 66:5 - Come and see the works of God, Who is awesome in His deeds toward the sons of men.

Ps. 68:35 - O God, You are awesome from Your sanctuary. The God of Israel Himself gives strength and power to the people. Blessed be God!

Ps. 89:7 - A God greatly feared in the council of the holy ones, And awesome above all those who are around Him?

Ps. 99:3 - Let them praise Your great and awesome name; Holy is He.

Ps. 106:22 - Wonders in the land of Ham And awesome things by the Red Sea.

Ps. 111:9 - He has sent redemption to His people; He has ordained His covenant forever; Holy and awesome is His name.

Ps. 145:6 - Men shall speak of the power of Your awesome acts, And I will tell of Your greatness.

BLAMELESS

Ps. 18:23 - I was also blameless with Him, And I kept myself from my iniquity.

Ps. 18:25 - With the kind You show Yourself kind; With the blameless You show Yourself blameless.

Ps. 18:30 - As for God, His way is blameless; The word of the Lord is tried; He is a shield to all who take refuge in Him.

Ps. 18:32 - The God who girds me with strength And makes my way blameless?

Ps. 19:13 - Also keep back Your servant from presumptuous sins; Let them not rule over me; Then I will be blameless, And I shall be acquitted of great transgression.

Ps. 37:18 - The Lord knows the days of the blameless, And their inheritance will be forever.

Ps. 37:37 - Mark the blameless man, and behold the upright; For the man of peace will have a posterity.

Ps. 51:4 - Against You, You only, I have sinned And done what is evil in Your sight, So that You are justified when You speak And blameless when You judge.

Ps. 64:4 - To shoot from concealment at the blameless; Suddenly they shoot at him, and do not fear.

Ps. 101:2 - I will give heed to the blameless way. When will You come to me? I will walk within my house in the integrity of my heart.

Ps. 101:6 - My eyes shall be upon the faithful of the land, that they may dwell with me; He who walks in a blameless way is the one who will minister to me.

Ps. 119:1 - How blessed are those whose way is blameless, Who walk in the law of the Lord.

Ps. 119:80 - May my heart be blameless in Your statutes, So that I will not be ashamed.

BLESSED

Ps. 1:1 - How blessed is the man who does not walk in the counsel of the wicked, Nor stand in the path of sinners, Nor sit in the seat of scoffers!

Ps. 2:12 - Do homage to the Son, that He not become angry, and you perish in the way, For His wrath may soon be kindled. How blessed are all who take refuge in Him!

Ps. 18:46 - The Lord lives, and blessed be my rock; And exalted be the God of my salvation.

Ps. 21:6 - For You make him most blessed forever; You make him joyful with gladness in Your presence.

Ps. 28:6 - Blessed be the Lord, Because He has heard the voice of my supplication.

Ps. 31:21 - Blessed be the Lord, For He has made marvelous His lovingkindness to me in a besieged city.

Ps. 32:1 - How blessed is he whose transgression is forgiven, Whose sin is covered!

Ps. 32:2 - How blessed is the man to whom the Lord does not impute iniquity, And in whose spirit there is no deceit!

Ps. 33:12 - Blessed is the nation whose God is the Lord, The people whom He has chosen for His own inheritance.

Ps. 34:8 - O taste and see that the Lord is good; How blessed is the man who takes refuge in Him!

Ps. 37:22 - For those blessed by Him will inherit the land, But those cursed by Him will be cut off.

Ps. 40:4 - How blessed is the man who has made the Lord his trust, And has not turned to the proud, nor to those who lapse into falsehood.

Ps. 41:1 - How blessed is he who considers the helpless; The Lord will deliver him in a day of trouble.

Ps. 41:2 - The Lord will protect him and keep him alive, And he shall be called blessed upon the earth; And do not give him over to the desire of his enemies.

Ps. 41:13 - Blessed be the Lord, the God of Israel, From everlasting to everlasting. Amen and Amen.

Ps. 45:2 - You are fairer than the sons of men; Grace is poured upon Your lips; Therefore God has blessed You forever.

Ps. 65:4 - How blessed is the one whom You choose and bring near to You To dwell in Your courts. We will be satisfied with the goodness of Your house, Your holy temple.

Ps. 66:20 - Blessed be God, Who has not turned away my prayer Nor His lovingkindness from me.

Ps. 68:19 - Blessed be the Lord, who daily bears our burden, The God who is our salvation.

Ps. 68:35 - O God, You are awesome from Your sanctuary. The God of Israel Himself gives strength and power to the people. Blessed be God!

Ps. 72:17 - May his name endure forever; May his name increase as long as the sun shines; And let men bless themselves by him; Let all nations call him blessed.

Ps. 72:18 - Blessed be the Lord God, the God of Israel, Who alone works wonders.

Ps. 72:19 - And blessed be His glorious name forever; And may the whole earth be filled with His glory. Amen, and Amen.

Ps. 84:4 - How blessed are those who dwell in Your house! They are ever praising You.

Ps. 84:5 - How blessed is the man whose strength is in You, In whose heart are the highways to Zion!

Ps. 84:12 - O Lord of hosts, How blessed is the man who trusts in You!

Ps. 89:15 - How blessed are the people who know the joyful sound! O Lord, they walk in the light of Your countenance.

Ps. 89:52 - Blessed be the Lord forever! Amen and Amen.

Ps. 94:12 - Blessed is the man whom You chasten, O Lord, And whom You teach out of Your law.

Ps. 106:3 - How blessed are those who keep justice, Who practice righteousness at all times!

Ps. 106:48 Blessed be the Lord, the God of Israel, From everlasting even to everlasting. And let all the people say, "Amen." Praise the Lord!

Ps. 112:1 - Praise the Lord! How blessed is the man who fears the Lord, Who greatly delights in His commandments.

Ps. 112:2 - His descendants will be mighty on earth; The generation of the upright will be blessed.

Ps. 113:2 - Blessed be the name of the Lord From this time forth and forever.

Ps. 115:15 - May you be blessed of the Lord, Maker of heaven and earth.

Ps. 118:26 - Blessed is the one who comes in the name of the Lord; We have blessed you from the house of the Lord.

Ps. 119:1 - How blessed are those whose way is blameless, Who walk in the law of the Lord.

Ps. 119:2 - How blessed are those who observe His testimonies, Who seek Him with all their heart.

Ps. 119:12 - Blessed are You, O Lord; Teach me Your statutes.

Ps. 124:6 - Blessed be the Lord, Who has not given us to be torn by their teeth.

Ps. 127:5 - How blessed is the man whose quiver is full of them; They will not be ashamed When they speak with their enemies in the gate.

Ps. 128:1 - How blessed is everyone who fears the Lord, Who walks in His ways.

Ps. 128:4 - Behold, for thus shall the man be blessed Who fears the Lord.

Ps. 135:21 - Blessed be the Lord from Zion, Who dwells in Jerusalem. Praise the Lord!

Ps. 137:8 - O daughter of Babylon, you devastated one, How blessed will be the one who repays you With the recompense with which you have repaid us.

Ps. 137:9 - How blessed will be the one who seizes and dashes your little ones Against the rock.

Ps. 144:1 - Blessed be the Lord, my rock, Who trains my hands for war, And my fingers for battle.

Ps. 144:15 - How blessed are the people who are so situated; How blessed are the people whose God is the Lord!

Ps. 146:5 - How blessed is he whose help is the God of Jacob, Whose hope is in the Lord his God.

Ps. 147:13 - For He has strengthened the bars of your gates; He has blessed your sons within you.

BOUNTIFULLY

Ps. 13:6 - I will sing to the Lord, Because He has dealt bountifully with me.

Ps. 116:7 - Return to your rest, O my soul, For the Lord has dealt bountifully with you.

Ps. 119:17 - Deal bountifully with Your servant, That I may live and keep Your word.

Ps. 142:7 - Bring my soul out of prison, So that I may give thanks to Your name; The righteous will surround me, For You will deal bountifully with me.

CONFIDENCE

Ps. 71:5 - For You are my hope; O Lord God, You are my confidence from my youth.

Ps. 78:7 - That they should put their confidence in God And not forget the works of God, But keep His commandments.

COUNSEL

Ps. 1:1 - How blessed is the man who does not walk in the counsel of the wicked, Nor stand in the path of sinners, Nor sit in the seat of scoffers!

Ps. 2:2 - The kings of the earth take their stand And the rulers take counsel together Against the Lord and against His Anointed.

Ps. 13:2 - How long shall I take counsel in my soul, Having sorrow in my heart all the day? How long will my enemy be exalted over me?

Ps. 14:6 - You would put to shame the counsel of the afflicted, But the Lord is his refuge.

Ps. 20:4 - May He grant you your heart's desire And fulfill all your counsel!

Ps. 31:13 - For I have heard the slander of many, Terror is on every side; While they took counsel together against me, They schemed to take away my life.

Ps. 32:8 - I will instruct you and teach you in the way which you should go; I will counsel you with My eye upon you.

Ps. 33:10 - The Lord nullifies the counsel of the nations; He frustrates the plans of the peoples.

Ps. 33:11 - The counsel of the Lord stands forever, The plans of His heart from generation to generation.

Ps. 64:2 - Hide me from the secret counsel of evildoers, From the tumult of those who do iniquity.

Ps. 73:24 - With Your counsel You will guide me, And afterward receive me to glory.

Ps. 106:13 - They quickly forgot His works; They did not wait for His counsel.

Ps. 106:43 - Many times He would deliver them; They, however, were rebellious in their counsel, And so sank down in their iniquity.

Ps. 107:11 - Because they had rebelled against the words of God And spurned the counsel of the Most High.

COUNTENANCE

Ps. 4:6 - Many are saying, "Who will show us any good?" Lift up the light of Your countenance upon us, O Lord!

Ps. 10:4 - The wicked, in the haughtiness of his countenance, does not seek Him. All his thoughts are, "There is no God."

Ps. 42:11 - Why are you in despair, O my soul? And why have you become disturbed within me? Hope in

God, for I shall yet praise Him, The help of my countenance and my God.

Ps. 43:5 - Why are you in despair, O my soul? And why are you disturbed within me? Hope in God, for I shall again praise Him, The help of my countenance and my God.

Ps. 80:16 - It is burned with fire, it is cut down; They perish at the rebuke of Your countenance.

Ps. 89:15 - How blessed are the people who know the joyful sound! O Lord, they walk in the light of Your countenance.

COURAGE

Ps. 27:14 - Wait for the Lord; Be strong and let your heart take courage; Yes, wait for the Lord.

Ps. 31:24 - Be strong and let your heart take courage, All you who hope in the Lord.

CRY

Ps. 5:2 - Heed the sound of my cry for help, my King and my God, For to You I pray.

Ps. 9:12 - For He who requires blood remembers them; He does not forget the cry of the afflicted.

Ps. 17:1 - Hear a just cause, O Lord, give heed to my cry; Give ear to my prayer, which is not from deceitful lips.

Ps. 18:6 - In my distress I called upon the Lord, And cried to my God for help; He heard my voice out of His temple, And my cry for help before Him came into His ears.

Ps. 22:2 - O my God, I cry by day, but You do not answer; And by night, but I have no rest.

Ps. 27:7 - Hear, O Lord, when I cry with my voice, And be gracious to me and answer me.

Ps. 28:2 - Hear the voice of my supplications when I cry to You for help, When I lift up my hands toward Your holy sanctuary.

Ps. 34:15 - The eyes of the Lord are toward the righteous and His ears are open to their cry.

Ps. 34:17 - The righteous cry, and the Lord hears And delivers them out of all their troubles.

Ps. 39:12 - Hear my prayer, O Lord, and give ear to my cry; Do not be silent at my tears; For I am a stranger with You, A sojourner like all my fathers.

Ps. 40:1 - I waited patiently for the Lord; And He inclined to me and heard my cry.

Ps. 57:2 - I will cry to God Most High, To God who accomplishes all things for me.

Ps. 61:1 - Hear my cry, O God; Give heed to my prayer.

Ps. 77:1 - My voice rises to God, and I will cry aloud; My voice rises to God, and He will hear me.

Ps. 86:3 - Be gracious to me, O Lord, For to You I cry all day long.

Ps. 88:2 - Let my prayer come before You; Incline Your ear to my cry!

Ps. 89:26 - He will cry to Me, 'You are my Father, My God, and the rock of my salvation.'

Ps. 102:1 - Hear my prayer, O Lord! And let my cry for help come to You.

Ps. 106:44 - Nevertheless He looked upon their distress When He heard their cry.

Ps. 119:147 - I rise before dawn and cry for help; I wait for Your words.

Ps. 119:169 - Let my cry come before You, O Lord; Give me understanding according to Your word.

Ps. 142:1 - I cry aloud with my voice to the Lord; I make supplication with my voice to the Lord.

Ps. 142:6 - Give heed to my cry, For I am brought very low; Deliver me from my persecutors, For they are too strong for me.

Ps. 145:19 - He will fulfill the desire of those who fear Him; He will also hear their cry and will save them.

Ps. 147:9 - He gives to the beast its food, And to the young ravens which cry.

DELIVER

Ps. 7:1 - O Lord my God, in You I have taken refuge; Save me from all those who pursue me, and deliver me.

Ps. 7:2 - Or he will tear my soul like a lion, Dragging me away, while there is none to deliver.

Ps. 17:13 - Arise, O Lord, confront him, bring him low; Deliver my soul from the wicked with Your sword.

Ps. 22:8 - Commit yourself to the Lord; let Him deliver him; Let Him rescue him, because He delights in him.

Ps. 22:20 - Deliver my soul from the sword, My only life from the power of the dog.

Ps. 25:20 - Guard my soul and deliver me; Do not let me be ashamed, for I take refuge in You.

Ps. 27:12 - Do not deliver me over to the desire of my adversaries, For false witnesses have risen against me, And such as breathe out violence.

Ps. 31:1 - In You, O Lord, I have taken refuge; Let me never be ashamed; In Your righteousness deliver me.

Ps. 31:15 - My times are in Your hand; Deliver me from the hand of my enemies and from those who persecute me.

Ps. 33:17 - A horse is a false hope for victory; Nor does it deliver anyone by its great strength.

Ps. 33:19 - To deliver their soul from death And to keep them alive in famine.

Ps. 39:8 – Deliver me from all my transgressions; Make me not the reproach of the foolish.

Ps. 40:13 - Be pleased, O Lord, to deliver me; Make haste, O Lord, to help me.

Ps. 41:1 - How blessed is he who considers the helpless; The Lord will deliver him in a day of trouble.

Ps. 43:1 - Vindicate me, O God, and plead my case against an ungodly nation; O deliver me from the deceitful and unjust man!

Ps. 50:22 - Now consider this, you who forget God, Or I will tear you in pieces, and there will be none to deliver.

Ps. 51:14 - Deliver me from bloodguiltiness, O God, the God of my salvation; Then my tongue will joyfully sing of Your righteousness.

Ps. 59:1 - Deliver me from my enemies, O my God; Set me securely on high away from those who rise up against me.

Ps. 59:2 - Deliver me from those who do iniquity And save me from men of bloodshed.

Ps. 69:14 - Deliver me from the mire and do not let me sink; May I be delivered from my foes and from the deep waters.

Ps. 70:1 - O God, hasten to deliver me; O Lord, hasten to my help!

Ps. 71:2 - In Your righteousness deliver me and rescue me; Incline Your ear to me and save me.

Ps. 71:11 - Saying, "God has forsaken him; Pursue and seize him, for there is no one to deliver."

Ps. 72:12 - For he will deliver the needy when he cries for help, The afflicted also, and him who has no helper.

Ps. 74:19 - Do not deliver the soul of Your turtledove to the wild beast; Do not forget the life of Your afflicted forever.

Ps. 79:9 - Help us, O God of our salvation, for the glory of Your name; And deliver us and forgive our sins for Your name's sake.

Ps. 82:4 - Rescue the weak and needy; Deliver them out of the hand of the wicked.

Ps. 89:48 - What man can live and not see death? Can he deliver his soul from the power of Sheol?

Ps. 91:14 - Because he has loved Me, therefore I will deliver him; I will set him securely on high, because he has known My name.

Ps. 106:43 - Many times He would deliver them; They, however, were rebellious in their counsel, And so sank down in their iniquity.

Ps. 109:21 - But You, O God, the Lord, deal kindly with me for Your name's sake; Because Your lovingkindness is good, deliver me.

Ps. 119:170 - Let my supplication come before You; Deliver me according to Your word.

Ps. 120:2 - Deliver my soul, O Lord, from lying lips., From a deceitful tongue.

Ps. 142:6 - Give heed to my cry, For I am brought very low; Deliver me from my persecutors, For they are too strong for me.

Ps. 143:9 - Deliver me, O Lord, from my enemies; I take refuge in You.

Ps. 144:7 - Stretch forth Your hand from on high; Rescue me and deliver me out of great waters, Out of the hand of aliens

Ps. 144:11 - Rescue me and deliver me out of the hand of aliens, Whose mouth speaks deceit And whose right hand is a right hand of falsehood.

DWELL

Ps. 4:8 - In peace I will both lie down and sleep, For You alone, O Lord, make me to dwell in safety.

Ps. 15:1 - O Lord, who may abide in Your tent? Who may dwell on Your holy hill?

Ps. 16:9 - Therefore my heart is glad and my glory rejoices; My flesh also will dwell securely.

Ps. 23:6 - Surely goodness and lovingkindness will follow me all the days of my life, And I will dwell in the house of the Lord forever.

Ps. 24:1 - The earth is the Lord's, and all it contains, The world, and those who dwell in it.

Ps. 27:4 - One thing I have asked from the Lord, that I shall seek: That I may dwell in the house of the Lord all the days of my life, To behold the beauty of the Lord And to meditate in His temple.

Ps. 37:3 - Trust in the Lord and do good; Dwell in the land and cultivate faithfulness.

Ps. 37:29 - The righteous will inherit the land And dwell in it forever.

Ps. 61:4 - Let me dwell in Your tent forever; Let me take refuge in the shelter of Your wings.

Ps. 65:4 - How blessed is the one whom You choose and bring near to You To dwell in Your courts. We will be satisfied with the goodness of Your house, Your holy temple.

Ps. 65:8 - They who dwell in the ends of the earth stand in awe of Your signs; You make the dawn and the sunset shout for joy.

Ps. 68:6 - God makes a home for the lonely; He leads out the prisoners into prosperity, Only the rebellious dwell in a parched land.

Ps. 68:16 - Why do you look with envy, O mountains with many peaks, At the mountain which God has desired for His abode? Surely the Lord will dwell there forever.

Ps. 68:18 - You have ascended on high, You have led captive Your captives; You have received gifts among men, Even among the rebellious also, that the Lord God may dwell there.

Ps. 69:25 - May their camp be desolate; May none dwell in their tents.

Ps. 69:35 - For God will save Zion and build the cities of Judah, That they may dwell there and possess it.

Ps. 69:36 - The descendants of His servants will inherit it, And those who love His name will dwell in it.

Ps. 75:3 - The earth and all who dwell in it melt; It is I who have firmly set its pillars.

Ps. 78:55 - He also drove out the nations before them And apportioned them for an inheritance by measurement, And made the tribes of Israel dwell in their tents.

Ps. 84:4 - How blessed are those who dwell in Your house! They are ever praising You.

Ps. 84:10 - For a day in Your courts is better than a thousand outside. I would rather stand at the threshold of the house of my God Than dwell in the tents of wickedness.

Ps. 85:9 - Surely His salvation is near to those who fear Him, That glory may dwell in our land.

Ps. 98:7 - Let the sea roar and all it contains, The world and those who dwell in it.

Ps. 101:6 - My eyes shall be upon the faithful of the land, that they may dwell with me; He who walks in a blameless way is the one who will minister to me.

Ps. 101:7 - He who practices deceit shall not dwell within my house; He who speaks falsehood shall not maintain his position before me.

Ps. 104:12 - Beside them the birds of the heavens dwell; They lift up their voices among the branches.

Ps. 107:34 - A fruitful land into a salt waste, Because of the wickedness of those who dwell in it.

Ps. 107:36 - And there He makes the hungry to dwell, So that they may establish an inhabited city.

Ps. 120:5 - Woe is me, for I sojourn in Meshech, For I dwell among the tents of Kedar!

Ps. 132:14 - This is My resting place forever; Here I will dwell, for I have desired it.

Ps. 133:1 - Behold, how good and how pleasant it is For brothers to dwell together in unity!

Ps. 139:9 - If I take the wings of the dawn, If I dwell in the remotest part of the sea.

Ps. 140:13 - Surely the righteous will give thanks to Your name; The upright will dwell in Your presence.

Ps. 143:3 - For the enemy has persecuted my soul; He has crushed my life to the ground; He has made me dwell in dark places, like those who have long been dead.

EVERLASTING

Ps. 41:13 - Blessed be the Lord, the God of Israel, From everlasting to everlasting. Amen and Amen.

Ps. 78:66 - He drove His adversaries backward; He put on them an everlasting reproach.

Ps. 90:2 - Before the mountains were born Or You gave birth to the earth and the world, Even from everlasting to everlasting, You are God.

Ps. 93:2 - Your throne is established from of old; You are from everlasting.

Ps. 100:5 - For the Lord is good; His lovingkindness is everlasting And His faithfulness to all generations.

Ps. 103:17 - But the lovingkindness of the Lord is from everlasting to everlasting on those who fear Him, And His righteousness to children's children.

Ps. 105:10 - Then He confirmed it to Jacob for a statute, To Israel as an everlasting covenant.

Ps. 106:1 - Praise the Lord! Oh give thanks to the Lord, for He is good; For His lovingkindness is everlasting.

Ps. 106:48 - Blessed be the Lord, the God of Israel, From everlasting even to everlasting. And let all the people say, "Amen." Praise the Lord!

Ps. 107:1 - Oh give thanks to the Lord, for He is good, For His lovingkindness is everlasting.

Ps. 117:2 - For His lovingkindness is great toward us, And the truth of the Lord is everlasting. Praise the Lord!

Ps. 118:1 - Give thanks to the Lord, for He is good; For His lovingkindness is everlasting.

Ps. 118:2 - Oh let Israel say, "His lovingkindness is everlasting."

Ps. 118:3 - Oh let the house of Aaron say, "His lovingkindness is everlasting."

Ps. 118:4 - Oh let those who fear the Lord say, "His lovingkindness is everlasting."

Ps. 118:29 - Give thanks to the Lord, for He is good; For His lovingkindness is everlasting.

Ps. 119:142 - Your righteousness is an everlasting righteousness, And Your law is truth.

Ps. 119:160 - The sum of Your word is truth, And every one of Your righteous ordinances is everlasting.

Ps. 135:13 - Your name, O Lord, is everlasting, Your remembrance, O Lord, throughout all generations.

Ps. 136:1 - Give thanks to the Lord, for He is good, For His lovingkindness is everlasting.

Ps. 136:2 - Give thanks to the God of gods, For His lovingkindness is everlasting.

Ps. 136:3 - Give thanks to the Lord of lords, For His lovingkindness is everlasting.

Ps. 136:4 - To Him who alone does great wonders, For His lovingkindness is everlasting.

Ps. 136:5 - To Him who made the heavens with skill, For His lovingkindness is everlasting.

Ps. 136:6 - To Him who spread out the earth above the waters, For His lovingkindness is everlasting.

Ps. 136:7 - To Him who made the great lights, For His lovingkindness is everlasting.

Ps. 136:8 - The sun to rule by day, For His lovingkindness is everlasting.

Ps. 136:9 - The moon and stars to rule by night, For His lovingkindness is everlasting.

Ps. 136:10 - To Him who smote the Egyptians in their firstborn, For His lovingkindness is everlasting.

Ps. 136:11 - And brought Israel out from their midst, For His lovingkindness is everlasting.

Ps. 136:12 - With a strong hand and an outstretched arm, For His lovingkindness is everlasting.

Ps. 136:13 - To Him who divided the Red Sea asunder, For His lovingkindness is everlasting.

Ps. 136:14 - And made Israel pass through the midst of it, For His lovingkindness is everlasting.

Ps. 136:15 - But He overthrew Pharaoh and his army in the Red Sea, For His lovingkindness is everlasting.

Ps. 136:16 - To Him who led His people through the wilderness, For His lovingkindness is everlasting.

Ps. 136:17 - To Him who smote great kings, For His lovingkindness is everlasting.

Ps. 136:18 - And slew mighty kings, For His lovingkindness is everlasting.

Ps. 136:19 - Sihon, king of the Amorites, For His lovingkindness is everlasting,

Ps. 136:20 - And Og, king of Bashan, For His lovingkindness is everlasting.

Ps. 136:21 - And gave their land as a heritage, For His lovingkindness is everlasting.

Ps. 136:22 - Even a heritage to Israel His servant, For His lovingkindness is everlasting.

Ps. 136:23 - Who remembered us in our low estate, For His lovingkindness is everlasting.

Ps. 136:24 - And has rescued us from our adversaries, For His lovingkindness is everlasting.

Ps. 136:25 - Who gives food to all flesh, For His lovingkindness is everlasting.

Ps. 136:26 - Give thanks to the God of heaven, For His lovingkindness is everlasting.

Ps. 138:8 - The Lord will accomplish what concerns me; Your lovingkindness, O Lord, is everlasting; Do not forsake the works of Your hands.

Ps. 139:24 - And see if there be any hurtful way in me, And lead me in the everlasting way.

Ps. 145:13 - Your kingdom is an everlasting kingdom, And Your dominion endures throughout all generations.

EXALTED

Ps. 12:8 - The wicked strut about on every side When vileness is exalted among the sons of men.

Ps. 13:2 - How long shall I take counsel in my soul, Having sorrow in my heart all the day? How long will my enemy be exalted over me?

Ps. 18:46 - The Lord lives, and blessed be my rock; And exalted be the God of my salvation.

Ps. 21:13 - Be exalted, O Lord, in Your strength; We will sing and praise Your power.

Ps. 46:10 - Cease striving and know that I am God; I will be exalted among the nations, I will be exalted in the earth.

Ps. 47:9 - The princes of the people have assembled themselves as the people of the God of Abraham, For the shields of the earth belong to God; He is highly exalted.

Ps. 55:12 - For it is not an enemy who reproaches me, Then I could bear it; Nor is it one who hates me who has exalted himself against me, Then I could hide myself from him.

Ps. 57:5 - Be exalted above the heavens, O God; Let Your glory be above all the earth.

Ps. 57:11 - Be exalted above the heavens, O God; Let Your glory be above all the earth.

Ps. 83:2 - For behold, Your enemies make an uproar, And those who hate You have exalted themselves.

Ps. 89:13 You have a strong arm; Your hand is mighty, Your right hand is exalted.

Ps. 89:16 - In Your name they rejoice all the day, And by Your righteousness they are exalted.

Ps. 89:17 - For You are the glory of their strength, And by Your favor our horn is exalted.

Ps. 89:19 - Once You spoke in vision to Your godly ones, And said, "I have given help to one who is mighty; I have exalted one chosen from the people."

Ps. 89:24 - My faithfulness and My lovingkindness will be with him, And in My name his horn will be exalted.

Ps. 89:42 - You have exalted the right hand of his adversaries; You have made all his enemies rejoice.

Ps. 92:10 - But You have exalted my horn like that of the wild ox; I have been anointed with fresh oil.

Ps. 97:9 - For You are the Lord Most High over all the earth; You are exalted far above all gods.

Ps. 99:2 - The Lord is great in Zion, And He is exalted above all the peoples.

Ps. 108:5 - Be exalted, O God, above the heavens, And Your glory above all the earth.

Ps. 112:9 - He has given freely to the poor, His righteousness endures forever; His horn will be exalted in honor.

Ps. 118:16 - The right hand of the Lord is exalted; The right hand of the Lord does valiantly.

Ps. 138:6 - For though the Lord is exalted, Yet He regards the lowly, But the haughty He knows from afar.

Ps. 140:8 - Do not grant, O Lord, the desires of the wicked; Do not promote his evil device, that they not be exalted.

Ps. 148:13 - Let them praise the name of the Lord, For His name alone is exalted; His glory is above earth and heaven.

FACE

Ps. 10:11 - He says to himself, "God has forgotten; He has hidden His face; He will never see it."

Ps. 11:7 - For the Lord is righteous, He loves righteousness; The upright will behold His face.

Ps. 13:1 - How long, O Lord? Will You forget me forever? How long will You hide Your face from me?

Ps. 17:15 - As for me, I shall behold Your face in righteousness; I will be satisfied with Your likeness when I awake.

Ps. 22:24 - For He has not despised nor abhorred the affliction of the afflicted; Nor has He hidden His face from him; But when he cried to Him for help, He heard.

Ps. 24:6 - This is the generation of those who seek Him, Who seek Your face— even Jacob.

Ps. 27:8 - When You said, "Seek My face," my heart said to You, "Your face, O Lord, I shall seek."

Ps. 27:9 - Do not hide Your face from me, Do not turn Your servant away in anger; You have been my help;

Do not abandon me nor forsake me, O God of my salvation!

Ps. 30:7 - O Lord, by Your favor You have made my mountain to stand strong; You hid Your face, I was dismayed.

Ps. 31:16 - Make Your face to shine upon Your servant; Save me in Your lovingkindness.

Ps. 34:16 - The face of the Lord is against evildoers, To cut off the memory of them from the earth.

Ps. 44:24 - Why do You hide Your face And forget our affliction and our oppression?

Ps. 51:9 - Hide Your face from my sins And blot out all my iniquities.

Ps. 67:1 - God be gracious to us and bless us, And cause His face to shine upon us.

Ps. 69:7 - Because for Your sake I have borne reproach; Dishonor has covered my face.

Ps. 69:17 - And do not hide Your face from Your servant, For I am in distress; answer me quickly.

Ps. 80:3 - O God, restore us And cause Your face to shine upon us, and we will be saved.

Ps. 80:7 - O God of hosts, restore us And cause Your face to shine upon us, and we will be saved.

Ps. 80:19 - O Lord God of hosts, restore us; Cause Your face to shine upon us, and we will be saved.

Ps. 84:9 - Behold our shield, O God, And look upon the face of Your anointed.

Ps. 88:14 - O Lord, why do You reject my soul? Why do You hide Your face from me?

Ps. 102:2 - Do not hide Your face from me in the day of my distress; Incline Your ear to me; In the day when I call answer me quickly.

Ps. 104:15 - And wine which makes man's heart glad, So that he may make his face glisten with oil, And food which sustains man's heart.

Ps. 104:29 - You hide Your face, they are dismayed; You take away their spirit, they expire And return to their dust.

Ps. 104:30 - You send forth Your Spirit, they are created; And You renew the face of the ground.

Ps. 105:4 - Seek the Lord and His strength; Seek His face continually.

Ps. 119:135 - Make Your face shine upon Your servant, And teach me Your statutes.

Ps. 132:10 - For the sake of David Your servant, Do not turn away the face of Your anointed.

Ps. 143:7 - Answer me quickly, O Lord, my spirit fails; Do not hide Your face from me, Or I will become like those who go down to the pit.

FAITHFULNESS

Ps. 30:9 - What profit is there in my blood, if I go down to the pit? Will the dust praise You? Will it declare Your faithfulness?

Ps. 33:4 - For the word of the Lord is upright, And all His work is done in faithfulness.

Ps. 36:5 - Your lovingkindness, O Lord, extends to the heavens, Your faithfulness reaches to the skies.

Ps. 37:3 - Trust in the Lord and do good; Dwell in the land and cultivate faithfulness.

Ps. 40:10 - I have not hidden Your righteousness within my heart; I have spoken of Your faithfulness and Your salvation; I have not concealed Your lovingkindness and Your truth from the great congregation.

Ps. 54:5 - He will recompense the evil to my foes; Destroy them in Your faithfulness.

Ps. 88:11 - Will Your lovingkindness be declared in the grave, Your faithfulness in Abaddon?

Ps. 89:1 - I will sing of the lovingkindness of the Lord forever; To all generations I will make known Your faithfulness with my mouth.

Ps. 89:2 - For I have said, "Lovingkindness will be built up forever; In the heavens You will establish Your faithfulness."

Ps. 89:5 - The heavens will praise Your wonders, O Lord; Your faithfulness also in the assembly of the holy ones.

Ps. 89:8 - O Lord God of hosts, who is like You, O mighty Lord? Your faithfulness also surrounds You.

Ps. 89:24 - My faithfulness and My lovingkindness will be with him, And in My name his horn will be exalted.

Ps. 89:33 - But I will not break off My lovingkindness from him, Nor deal falsely in My faithfulness.

Ps. 89:49 - Where are Your former lovingkindnesses, O Lord, Which You swore to David in Your faithfulness?

Ps. 91:4 - He will cover you with His pinions, And under His wings you may seek refuge; His faithfulness is a shield and bulwark.

Ps. 92:2 - To declare Your lovingkindness in the morning And Your faithfulness by night.

Ps. 96:13 - Before the Lord, for He is coming, For He is coming to judge the earth. He will judge the world in righteousness And the peoples in His faithfulness.

Ps. 98:3 - He has remembered His lovingkindness and His faithfulness to the house of Israel; All the ends of the earth have seen the salvation of our God.

Ps. 100:5 - For the Lord is good; His lovingkindness is everlasting And His faithfulness to all generations.

Ps. 119:75 - I know, O Lord, that Your judgments are righteous, And that in faithfulness You have afflicted me.

Ps. 119:90 - Your faithfulness continues throughout all generations; You established the earth, and it stands.

Ps. 119:138 - You have commanded Your testimonies in righteousness And exceeding faithfulness.

Ps. 143:1 - Hear my prayer, O Lord, Give ear to my supplications! Answer me in Your faithfulness, in Your righteousness!

FORSAKE

Ps. 27:9 - Do not hide Your face from me, Do not turn Your servant away in anger; You have been my help; Do not abandon me nor forsake me, O God of my salvation!

Ps. 37:8 - Cease from anger and forsake wrath; Do not fret; it leads only to evildoing.

Ps. 37:28 - For the Lord loves justice And does not forsake His godly ones; They are preserved forever, But the descendants of the wicked will be cut off.

Ps. 38:21 - Do not forsake me, O Lord; O my God, do not be far from me!

Ps. 71:9 - Do not cast me off in the time of old age; Do not forsake me when my strength fails.

Ps. 71:18 - And even when I am old and gray, O God, do not forsake me, Until I declare Your strength to this generation, Your power to all who are to come.

Ps. 89:30 - If his sons forsake My law And do not walk in My judgments.

Ps. 94:14 - For the Lord will not abandon His people, Nor will He forsake His inheritance.

Ps. 119:8 - I shall keep Your statutes; Do not forsake me utterly!

Ps. 119:53 - Burning indignation has seized me because of the wicked, Who forsake Your law.

Ps. 119:87 - They almost destroyed me on earth, But as for me, I did not forsake Your precepts.

Ps. 138:8 - The Lord will accomplish what concerns me; Your lovingkindness, O Lord, is everlasting; Do not forsake the works of Your hands.

GENERATIONS

Ps. 10:6 - He says to himself, "I will not be moved; Throughout all generations I will not be in adversity."

Ps. 45:17 - I will cause Your name to be remembered in all generations; Therefore the peoples will give You thanks forever and ever.

Ps. 49:11 - Their inner thought is that their houses are forever And their dwelling places to all generations; They have called their lands after their own names.

Ps. 61:6 - You will prolong the king's life; His years will be as many generations.

Ps. 72:5 - Let them fear You while the sun endures, And as long as the moon, throughout all generations.

Ps. 79:13 - So we Your people and the sheep of Your pasture Will give thanks to You forever; To all generations we will tell of Your praise.

Ps. 85:5 - Will You be angry with us forever? Will You prolong Your anger to all generations?

Ps. 89:1 - I will sing of the lovingkindness of the Lord forever; To all generations I will make known Your faithfulness with my mouth.

Ps. 89:4 - I will establish your seed forever And build up your throne to all generations.

Ps. 90:1 - A Prayer of Moses, the man of God. Lord, You have been our dwelling place in all generations.

Ps. 100:5 - For the Lord is good; His lovingkindness is everlasting And His faithfulness to all generations.

Ps. 102:12 - But You, O Lord, abide forever, And Your name to all generations.

Ps. 102:24 - I say, "O my God, do not take me away in the midst of my days, Your years are throughout all generations.

Ps. 105:8 - He has remembered His covenant forever, The word which He commanded to a thousand generations.

Ps. 106:31 - And it was reckoned to him for righteousness, To all generations forever.

Ps. 119:90 - Your faithfulness continues throughout all generations; You established the earth, and it stands.

Ps. 135:13 - Your name, O Lord, is everlasting, Your remembrance, O Lord, throughout all generations.

Ps. 145:13 - Your kingdom is an everlasting kingdom, And Your dominion endures throughout all generations.

Ps. 146:10 - The Lord will reign forever, Your God, O Zion, to all generations. Praise the Lord!

GIRDED

Ps. 18:39 - For You have girded me with strength for battle; You have subdued under me those who rose up against me.

Ps. 30:11 - You have turned for me my mourning into dancing; You have loosed my sackcloth and girded me with gladness.

Ps. 65:6 - Who establishes the mountains by His strength, Being girded with might.

Ps. 93:1 - The Lord reigns, He is clothed with majesty; The Lord has clothed and girded Himself with strength; Indeed, the world is firmly established, it will not be moved.

GLORY

Ps. 3:3 - But You, O Lord, are a shield about me, My glory, and the One who lifts my head.

Ps. 7:5 - Let the enemy pursue my soul and overtake it; And let him trample my life down to the ground And lay my glory in the dust.

Ps. 8:5 - Yet You have made him a little lower than God, And You crown him with glory and majesty!

Ps. 16:9 - Therefore my heart is glad and my glory rejoices; My flesh also will dwell securely.

Ps. 19:1 - The heavens are telling of the glory of God; And their expanse is declaring the work of His hands.

Ps. 21:5 - His glory is great through Your salvation, Splendor and majesty You place upon him.

Ps. 24:7 - Lift up your heads, O gates, And be lifted up, O ancient doors, That the King of glory may come in!

Ps. 24:8 - Who is the King of glory? The Lord strong and mighty, The Lord mighty in battle.

Ps. 24:9 - Lift up your heads, O gates, And lift them up, O ancient doors, That the King of glory may come in!

Ps. 24:10 - Who is this King of glory? The Lord of hosts, He is the King of glory.

Ps. 26:8 - O Lord, I love the habitation of Your house And the place where Your glory dwells.

Ps. 29:1 - Ascribe to the Lord, O sons of the mighty, Ascribe to the Lord glory and strength.

Ps. 29:2 - Ascribe to the Lord the glory due to His name; Worship the Lord in holy array.

Ps. 29:3 - The voice of the Lord is upon the waters; The God of glory thunders, The Lord is over many waters.

Ps. 29:9 - The voice of the Lord makes the deer to calve And strips the forests bare; And in His temple everything says, "Glory!"

Ps. 37:20 - But the wicked will perish; And the enemies of the Lord will be like the glory of the pastures, They vanish — like smoke they vanish away.

Ps. 47:4 - He chooses our inheritance for us, The glory of Jacob whom He loves.

Ps. 49:16 - Do not be afraid when a man becomes rich, When the glory of his house is increased.

Ps. 49:17 - For when he dies he will carry nothing away; His glory will not descend after him.

Ps. 57:5 - Be exalted above the heavens, O God; Let Your glory be above all the earth.

Ps. 57:8 - Awake, my glory! Awake, harp and lyre! I will awaken the dawn.

Ps. 57:11 - Be exalted above the heavens, O God; Let Your glory be above all the earth.

Ps. 62:7 - On God my salvation and my glory rest; The rock of my strength, my refuge is in God.

Ps. 63:2 - Thus I have seen You in the sanctuary, To see Your power and Your glory.

Ps. 63:11 - But the king will rejoice in God; Everyone who swears by Him will glory, For the mouths of those who speak lies will be stopped.

Ps. 64:10 - The righteous man will be glad in the Lord and will take refuge in Him; And all the upright in heart will glory.

Ps. 66:2 - Sing the glory of His name; Make His praise glorious.

Ps. 71:8 - My mouth is filled with Your praise And with Your glory all day long.

Ps. 72:19 - And blessed be His glorious name forever; And may the whole earth be filled with His glory. Amen, and Amen.

Ps. 73:24 - With Your counsel You will guide me, And afterward receive me to glory.

Ps. 78:61 - And gave up His strength to captivity And His glory into the hand of the adversary.

Ps. 79:9 - Help us, O God of our salvation, for the glory of Your name; And deliver us and forgive our sins for Your name's sake.

Ps. 84:11 - For the Lord God is a sun and shield; The Lord gives grace and glory; No good thing does He withhold from those who walk uprightly.

Ps. 85:9 - Surely His salvation is near to those who fear Him, That glory may dwell in our land.

Ps. 89:17 - For You are the glory of their strength, And by Your favor our horn is exalted.

Ps. 96:3 - Tell of His glory among the nations, His wonderful deeds among all the peoples.

Ps. 96:7 - Ascribe to the Lord, O families of the peoples, Ascribe to the Lord glory and strength.

Ps. 96:8 - Ascribe to the Lord the glory of His name; Bring an offering and come into His courts.

Ps. 97:6 - The heavens declare His righteousness, And all the peoples have seen His glory.

Ps. 102:15 - So the nations will fear the name of the Lord And all the kings of the earth Your glory.

Ps. 102:16 - For the Lord has built up Zion; He has appeared in His glory.

Ps. 104:31 - Let the glory of the Lord endure forever; Let the Lord be glad in His works.

Ps. 105:3 - Glory in His holy name; Let the heart of those who seek the Lord be glad.

Ps. 106:5 - That I may see the prosperity of Your chosen ones, That I may rejoice in the gladness of Your nation, That I may glory with Your inheritance.

Ps. 106:20 - Thus they exchanged their glory For the image of an ox that eats grass.

Ps. 106:47 - Save us, O Lord our God, And gather us from among the nations, To give thanks to Your holy name And glory in Your praise.

Ps. 108:5 - Be exalted, O God, above the heavens, And Your glory above all the earth.

Ps. 113:4 - The Lord is high above all nations; His glory is above the heavens.

Ps. 115:1 - Not to us, O Lord, not to us, But to Your name give glory Because of Your lovingkindness, because of Your truth.

Ps. 138:5 - And they will sing of the ways of the Lord, For great is the glory of the Lord.

Ps. 145:11 - They shall speak of the glory of Your kingdom And talk of Your power.

Ps. 145:12 - To make known to the sons of men Your mighty acts And the glory of the majesty of Your kingdom.

Ps. 148:13 - Let them praise the name of the Lord, For His name alone is exalted; His glory is above earth and heaven.

Ps. 149:5 - Let the godly ones exult in glory; Let them sing for joy on their beds.

GRACIOUS

Ps. 4:1 - Answer me when I call, O God of my righteousness! You have relieved me in my distress; Be gracious to me and hear my prayer.

Ps. 6:2 - Be gracious to me, O Lord, for I am pining away; Heal me, O Lord, for my bones are dismayed.

Ps. 9:13 - Be gracious to me, O Lord; See my affliction from those who hate me, You who lift me up from the gates of death.

Ps. 25:16 - Turn to me and be gracious to me, For I am lonely and afflicted.

Ps. 26:11 - But as for me, I shall walk in my integrity; Redeem me, and be gracious to me.

Ps. 27:7 - Hear, O Lord, when I cry with my voice, And be gracious to me and answer me.

Ps. 30:10 - Hear, O Lord, and be gracious to me; O Lord, be my helper.

Ps. 31:9 - Be gracious to me, O Lord, for I am in distress; My eye is wasted away from grief, my soul and my body also.

Ps. 37:21 - The wicked borrows and does not pay back, But the righteous is gracious and gives.

Ps. 37:26 - All day long he is gracious and lends, And his descendants are a blessing.

Ps. 41:4 - As for me, I said, "O Lord, be gracious to me; Heal my soul, for I have sinned against You."

Ps. 41:10 - But You, O Lord, be gracious to me and raise me up, That I may repay them.

Ps. 51:1 - Be gracious to me, O God, according to Your lovingkindness; According to the greatness of Your compassion blot out my transgressions.

Ps. 56:1 - Be gracious to me, O God, for man has trampled upon me; Fighting all day long he oppresses me.

Ps. 57:1 - Be gracious to me, O God, be gracious to me, For my soul takes refuge in You; And in the shadow of Your wings I will take refuge Until destruction passes by.

Ps. 59:5 - You, O Lord God of hosts, the God of Israel, Awake to punish all the nations; Do not be gracious to any who are treacherous in iniquity.

Ps. 67:1 - God be gracious to us and bless us, And cause His face to shine upon us.

Ps. 77:9 - Has God forgotten to be gracious, Or has He in anger withdrawn His compassion?

Ps. 86:3 - Be gracious to me, O Lord, For to You I cry all day long.

Ps. 86:15 - But You, O Lord, are a God merciful and gracious, Slow to anger and abundant in lovingkindness and truth.

Ps. 86:16 - Turn to me, and be gracious to me; Oh grant Your strength to Your servant, And save the son of Your handmaid.

Ps. 102:13 - You will arise and have compassion on Zion; For it is time to be gracious to her, For the appointed time has come.

Ps. 103:8 - The Lord is compassionate and gracious, Slow to anger and abounding in lovingkindness.

Ps. 109:12 - Let there be none to extend lovingkindness to him, Nor any to be gracious to his fatherless children.

Ps. 111:4 - He has made His wonders to be remembered; The Lord is gracious and compassionate.

Ps. 112:4 - Light arises in the darkness for the upright; He is gracious and compassionate and righteous.

Ps. 112:5 - It is well with the man who is gracious and lends; He will maintain his cause in judgment.

Ps. 116:5 - Gracious is the Lord, and righteous; Yes, our God is compassionate.

Ps. 119:58 - I sought Your favor with all my heart; Be gracious to me according to Your word.

Ps. 119:132 - Turn to me and be gracious to me, After Your manner with those who love Your name.

Ps. 123:2 - Behold, as the eyes of servants look to the hand of their master, As the eyes of a maid to the hand of her mistress, So our eyes look to the Lord our God, Until He is gracious to us.

Ps. 123:3 - Be gracious to us, O Lord, be gracious to us, For we are greatly filled with contempt.

Ps. 145:8 - The Lord is gracious and merciful; Slow to anger and great in lovingkindness.

GUIDE
Ps. 31:3 - For You are my rock and my fortress; For Your name's sake You will lead me and guide me.

Ps. 48:14 - For such is God, Our God forever and ever; He will guide us until death.

Ps. 67:4 - Let the nations be glad and sing for joy; For You will judge the peoples with uprightness And guide the nations on the earth.

Ps. 73:24 - With Your counsel You will guide me, And afterward receive me to glory.

HEART

Ps. 4:4 - Tremble, and do not sin; Meditate in your heart upon your bed, and be still.

Ps. 4:7 - You have put gladness in my heart, More than when their grain and new wine abound.

Ps. 7:10 - My shield is with God, Who saves the upright in heart.

Ps. 9:1 - I will give thanks to the Lord with all my heart; I will tell of all Your wonders.

Ps. 10:3 - For the wicked boasts of his heart's desire, And the greedy man curses and spurns the Lord.

Ps. 10:17 - O Lord, You have heard the desire of the humble; You will strengthen their heart, You will incline Your ear.

Ps. 11:2 - For, behold, the wicked bend the bow, They make ready their arrow upon the string To shoot in darkness at the upright in heart.

Ps. 12:2 - They speak falsehood to one another; With flattering lips and with a double heart they speak.

Ps. 13:2 - How long shall I take counsel in my soul, Having sorrow in my heart all the day? How long will my enemy be exalted over me?

Ps. 13:5 - But I have trusted in Your lovingkindness; My heart shall rejoice in Your salvation.

Ps. 14:1 - The fool has said in his heart, "There is no God." They are corrupt, they have committed abominable deeds; There is no one who does good.

Ps. 15:2 - He who walks with integrity, and works righteousness, And speaks truth in his heart.

Ps. 16:9 - Therefore my heart is glad and my glory rejoices; My flesh also will dwell securely.

Ps. 17:3 You have tried my heart; You have visited me by night; You have tested me and You find nothing; I have purposed that my mouth will not transgress.

Ps. 17:10 - They have closed their unfeeling heart, With their mouth they speak proudly.

Ps. 19:8 - The precepts of the Lord are right, rejoicing the heart; The commandment of the Lord is pure, enlightening the eyes.

Ps. 19:14 - Let the words of my mouth and the meditation of my heart Be acceptable in Your sight, O Lord, my rock and my Redeemer.

Ps. 20:4 - May He grant you your heart's desire And fulfill all your counsel!

Ps. 21:2 - You have given him his heart's desire, And You have not withheld the request of his lips.

Ps. 22:14 - I am poured out like water, And all my bones are out of joint; My heart is like wax; It is melted within me.

Ps. 22:26 - The afflicted will eat and be satisfied; Those who seek Him will praise the Lord. Let your heart live forever!

Ps. 24:4 - He who has clean hands and a pure heart, Who has not lifted up his soul to falsehood And has not sworn deceitfully.

Ps. 25:17 - The troubles of my heart are enlarged; Bring me out of my distresses.

Ps. 26:2 - Examine me, O Lord, and try me; Test my mind and my heart.

Ps. 27:3 - Though a host encamp against me, My heart will not fear; Though war arise against me, In spite of this I shall be confident.

Ps. 27:8 - When You said, "Seek My face," my heart said to You, "Your face, O Lord, I shall seek."

Ps. 27:14 - Wait for the Lord; Be strong and let your heart take courage; Yes, wait for the Lord.

Ps. 28:7 - The Lord is my strength and my shield; My heart trusts in Him, and I am helped; Therefore my heart exults, And with my song I shall thank Him.

Ps. 31:24 - Be strong and let your heart take courage, All you who hope in the Lord.

Ps. 32:11 - Be glad in the Lord and rejoice, you righteous ones; And shout for joy, all you who are upright in heart.

Ps. 33:11 - The counsel of the Lord stands forever, The plans of His heart from generation to generation.

Ps. 33:21 For our heart rejoices in Him, Because we trust in His holy name.

Ps. 35:25 - Do not let them say in their heart, "Aha, our desire!" Do not let them say, "We have swallowed him up!"

Ps. 36:1 - Transgression speaks to the ungodly within his heart; There is no fear of God before his eyes.

Ps. 36:10 - O continue Your lovingkindness to those who know You, And Your righteousness to the upright in heart.

Ps. 37:4 - Delight yourself in the Lord; And He will give you the desires of your heart.

Ps. 37:15 - Their sword will enter their own heart, And their bows will be broken.

Ps. 37:31 - The law of his God is in his heart; His steps do not slip.

Ps. 38:8 - I am benumbed and badly crushed; I groan because of the agitation of my heart.

Ps. 38:10 - My heart throbs, my strength fails me; And the light of my eyes, even that has gone from me.

Ps. 39:3 - My heart was hot within me, While I was musing the fire burned; Then I spoke with my tongue.

Ps. 40:8 - I delight to do Your will, O my God; Your Law is within my heart.

Ps. 40:10 - I have not hidden Your righteousness within my heart; I have spoken of Your faithfulness and Your salvation; I have not concealed Your lovingkindness and Your truth from the great congregation.

Ps. 40:12 - For evils beyond number have surrounded me; My iniquities have overtaken me, so that I am not able to see; They are more numerous than the hairs of my head, And my heart has failed me.

Ps. 41:6 - And when he comes to see me, he speaks falsehood; His heart gathers wickedness to itself; When he goes outside, he tells it.

Ps. 44:18 - Our heart has not turned back, And our steps have not deviated from Your way.

Ps. 44:21 - Would not God find this out? For He knows the secrets of the heart.

Ps. 45:1 - My heart overflows with a good theme; I address my verses to the King; My tongue is the pen of a ready writer.

Ps. 45:5 - Your arrows are sharp; The peoples fall under You; Your arrows are in the heart of the King's enemies.

Ps. 46:2 - Therefore we will not fear, though the earth should change And though the mountains slip into the heart of the sea.

Ps. 49:3 - My mouth will speak wisdom, And the meditation of my heart will be understanding.

Ps. 51:10 - Create in me a clean heart, O God, And renew a steadfast spirit within me.

Ps. 51:17 - The sacrifices of God are a broken spirit; A broken and a contrite heart, O God, You will not despise.

Ps. 53:1 - The fool has said in his heart, "There is no God," They are corrupt, and have committed abominable injustice; There is no one who does good.

Ps. 55:4 - My heart is in anguish within me, And the terrors of death have fallen upon me.

Ps. 55:21 - His speech was smoother than butter, But his heart was war; His words were softer than oil, Yet they were drawn swords.

Ps. 57:7 - My heart is steadfast, O God, my heart is steadfast; I will sing, yes, I will sing praises!

Ps. 58:2 - No, in heart you work unrighteousness; On earth you weigh out the violence of your hands.

Ps. 61:2 - From the end of the earth I call to You when my heart is faint; Lead me to the rock that is higher than I.

Ps. 62:8 - Trust in Him at all times, O people; Pour out your heart before Him; God is a refuge for us.

Ps. 62:10 - Do not trust in oppression And do not vainly hope in robbery; If riches increase, do not set your heart upon them.

Ps. 64:6 - They devise injustices, saying, "We are ready with a well-conceived plot"; For the inward thought and the heart of a man are deep.

Ps. 64:10 - The righteous man will be glad in the Lord and will take refuge in Him; And all the upright in heart will glory.

Ps. 66:18 - If I regard wickedness in my heart, The Lord will not hear.

Ps. 69:20 - Reproach has broken my heart and I am so sick. And I looked for sympathy, but there was none, And for comforters, but I found none.

Ps. 69:32 - The humble have seen it and are glad; You who seek God, let your heart revive.

Ps. 73:1 - Surely God is good to Israel, To those who are pure in heart!

Ps. 73:7 - Their eye bulges from fatness; The imaginations of their heart run riot.

Ps. 73:13 - Surely in vain I have kept my heart pure And washed my hands in innocence.

Ps. 73:21 - When my heart was embittered And I was pierced within.

Ps. 73:26 - My flesh and my heart may fail, But God is the strength of my heart and my portion forever.

Ps. 74:8 - They said in their heart, "Let us completely subdue them." They have burned all the meeting places of God in the land.

Ps. 77:6 - I will remember my song in the night; I will meditate with my heart, And my spirit ponders.

Ps. 78:8 - And not be like their fathers, A stubborn and rebellious generation, A generation that did not prepare its heart And whose spirit was not faithful to God.

Ps. 78:18 - And in their heart they put God to the test By asking food according to their desire.

Ps. 78:37 - For their heart was not steadfast toward Him, Nor were they faithful in His covenant.

Ps. 78:72 - So he shepherded them according to the integrity of his heart, And guided them with his skillful hands.

Ps. 81:12 – So I gave them over to the stubbornness of their heart, To walk in their own devices.

Ps. 84:2 - My soul longed and even yearned for the courts of the Lord; My heart and my flesh sing for joy to the living God.

Ps. 84:5 - How blessed is the man whose strength is in You, In whose heart are the highways to Zion!

Ps. 86:11 - Teach me Your way, O Lord; I will walk in Your truth; Unite my heart to fear Your name.

Ps. 86:12 - I will give thanks to You, O Lord my God, with all my heart, And will glorify Your name forever.

Ps. 90:12 - So teach us to number our days, That we may present to You a heart of wisdom.

Ps. 94:15 - For judgment will again be righteous, And all the upright in heart will follow it.

Ps. 95:10 - For forty years I loathed that generation, And said they are a people who err in their heart, And they do not know My ways.

Ps. 97:11 - Light is sown like seed for the righteous And gladness for the upright in heart.

Ps. 101:2 - I will give heed to the blameless way. When will You come to me? I will walk within my house in the integrity of my heart.

Ps. 101:4 - A perverse heart shall depart from me; I will know no evil.

Ps. 101:5 - Whoever secretly slanders his neighbor, him I will destroy; No one who has a haughty look and an arrogant heart will I endure.

Ps. 102:4 - My heart has been smitten like grass and has withered away, Indeed, I forget to eat my bread.

Ps. 104:15 - And wine which makes man's heart glad, So that he may make his face glisten with oil, And food which sustains man's heart.

Ps. 105:3 - Glory in His holy name; Let the heart of those who seek the Lord be glad.

Ps. 105:25 - He turned their heart to hate His people, To deal craftily with His servants.

Ps. 107:12 - Therefore He humbled their heart with labor; They stumbled and there was none to help.

Ps. 108:1 - My heart is steadfast, O God; I will sing, I will sing praises, even with my soul.

Ps. 109:16 - Because he did not remember to show lovingkindness, But persecuted the afflicted and needy man, And the despondent in heart, to put them to death.

Ps. 109:22 - For I am afflicted and needy, And my heart is wounded within me.

Ps. 111:1 - Praise the Lord! I will give thanks to the Lord with all my heart, In the company of the upright and in the assembly.

Ps. 112:7 - He will not fear evil tidings; His heart is steadfast, trusting in the Lord.

Ps. 112:8 - His heart is upheld, he will not fear, Until he looks with satisfaction on his adversaries.

Ps. 119:2 - How blessed are those who observe His testimonies, Who seek Him with all their heart.

Ps. 119:7 - I shall give thanks to You with uprightness of heart, When I learn Your righteous judgments.

Ps. 119:10 - With all my heart I have sought You; Do not let me wander from Your commandments.

Ps. 119:11 - Your word I have treasured in my heart, That I may not sin against You.

Ps. 119:32 - I shall run the way of Your commandments, For You will enlarge my heart.

Ps. 119:34 - Give me understanding, that I may observe Your law And keep it with all my heart.

Ps. 119:36 - Incline my heart to Your testimonies And not to dishonest gain.

Ps. 119:58 - I sought Your favor with all my heart; Be gracious to me according to Your word.

Ps. 119:69 - The arrogant have forged a lie against me; With all my heart I will observe Your precepts.

Ps. 119:70 - Their heart is covered with fat, But I delight in Your law.

Ps. 119:80 - May my heart be blameless in Your statutes, So that I will not be ashamed.

Ps. 119:111 - I have inherited Your testimonies forever, For they are the joy of my heart.

Ps. 119:112 - I have inclined my heart to perform Your statutes Forever, even to the end.

Ps. 119:145 - I cried with all my heart; answer me, O Lord! I will observe Your statutes.

Ps. 119:161 - Princes persecute me without cause, But my heart stands in awe of Your words.

Ps. 131:1 - O Lord, my heart is not proud, nor my eyes haughty; Nor do I involve myself in great matters, Or in things too difficult for me.

Ps. 138:1 - I will give You thanks with all my heart; I will sing praises to You before the gods.

Ps. 139:23 - Search me, O God, and know my heart; Try me and know my anxious thoughts.

Ps. 141:4 - Do not incline my heart to any evil thing, To practice deeds of wickedness With men who do iniquity; And do not let me eat of their delicacies.

HELP

Ps. 5:2 - Heed the sound of my cry for help, my King and my God, For to You I pray.

Ps. 12:1 - Help, Lord, for the godly man ceases to be, For the faithful disappear from among the sons of men.

Ps. 18:6 - In my distress I called upon the Lord, And cried to my God for help; He heard my voice out of His temple, And my cry for help before Him came into His ears.

Ps. 18:41 - They cried for help, but there was none to save, Even to the Lord, but He did not answer them.

Ps. 20:2 - May He send you help from the sanctuary And support you from Zion!

Ps. 22:11 - Be not far from me, for trouble is near; For there is none to help.

Ps. 22:19 - But You, O Lord, be not far off; O You my help, hasten to my assistance.

Ps. 22:24 - For He has not despised nor abhorred the affliction of the afflicted; Nor has He hidden His face from him; But when he cried to Him for help, He heard.

Ps. 27:9 - Do not hide Your face from me, Do not turn Your servant away in anger; You have been my help; Do not abandon me nor forsake me, O God of my salvation!

Ps. 28:2 - Hear the voice of my supplications when I cry to You for help, When I lift up my hands toward Your holy sanctuary.

Ps. 30:2 - O Lord my God, I cried to You for help, and You healed me.

Ps. 33:20 - Our soul waits for the Lord; He is our help and our shield.

Ps. 35:2 - Take hold of buckler and shield And rise up for my help.

Ps. 38:22 - Make haste to help me, O Lord, my salvation!

Ps. 40:13 - Be pleased, O Lord, to deliver me; Make haste, O Lord, to help me.

Ps. 40:17 - Since I am afflicted and needy, Let the Lord be mindful of me. You are my help and my deliverer; Do not delay, O my God.

Ps. 42:5 - Why are you in despair, O my soul? And why have you become disturbed within me? Hope in God, for I shall again praise Him For the help of His presence.

Ps. 42:11 - Why are you in despair, O my soul? And why have you become disturbed within me? Hope in God, for I shall yet praise Him, The help of my countenance and my God.

Ps. 43:5 - Why are you in despair, O my soul? And why are you disturbed within me? Hope in God, for I shall again praise Him, The help of my countenance and my God.

Ps. 44:26 - Rise up, be our help, And redeem us for the sake of Your lovingkindness.

Ps. 46:1 - God is our refuge and strength, A very present help in trouble.

Ps. 46:5 - God is in the midst of her, she will not be moved; God will help her when morning dawns.

Ps. 59:4 - For no guilt of mine, they run and set themselves against me. Arouse Yourself to help me, and see!

Ps. 60:11 - O give us help against the adversary, For deliverance by man is in vain.

Ps. 63:7 - For You have been my help, And in the shadow of Your wings I sing for joy.

Ps. 70:1 - O God, hasten to deliver me; O Lord, hasten to my help!

Ps. 70:5 - But I am afflicted and needy; Hasten to me, O God! You are my help and my deliverer; O Lord, do not delay.

Ps. 71:12 - O God, do not be far from me; O my God, hasten to my help!

Ps. 72:12 - For he will deliver the needy when he cries for help, The afflicted also, and him who has no helper.

Ps. 79:9 - Help us, O God of our salvation, for the glory of Your name; And deliver us and forgive our sins for Your name's sake.

Ps. 83:8 - Assyria also has joined with them; They have become a help to the children of Lot.

Ps. 88:13 - But I, O Lord, have cried out to You for help, And in the morning my prayer comes before You.

Ps. 89:19 - Once You spoke in vision to Your godly ones, And said, "I have given help to one who is mighty; I have exalted one chosen from the people."

Ps. 94:17 - If the Lord had not been my help, My soul would soon have dwelt in the abode of silence.

Ps. 102:1 - Hear my prayer, O Lord! And let my cry for help come to You.

Ps. 107:12 - Therefore He humbled their heart with labor; They stumbled and there was none to help.

Ps. 108:12 - Oh give us help against the adversary, For deliverance by man is in vain.

Ps. 109:26 - Help me, O Lord my God; Save me according to Your lovingkindness.

Ps. 115:9 - O Israel, trust in the Lord; He is their help and their shield.

Ps. 115:10 - O house of Aaron, trust in the Lord; He is their help and their shield.

Ps. 115:11 - You who fear the Lord, trust in the Lord; He is their help and their shield.

Ps. 118:7 - The Lord is for me among those who help me; Therefore I will look with satisfaction on those who hate me.

Ps. 119:86 - All Your commandments are faithful; They have persecuted me with a lie; help me!

Ps. 119:147 - I rise before dawn and cry for help; I wait for Your words.

Ps. 119:173 - Let Your hand be ready to help me, For I have chosen Your precepts.

Ps. 119:175 - Let my soul live that it may praise You, And let Your ordinances help me.

Ps. 121:1 - I will lift up my eyes to the mountains; From where shall my help come?

Ps. 121:2 - My help comes from the Lord, Who made heaven and earth.

Ps. 124:8 - Our help is in the name of the Lord, Who made heaven and earth.

Ps. 146:5 - How blessed is he whose help is the God of Jacob, Whose hope is in the Lord his God.

HOPE

Ps. 9:18 - For the needy will not always be forgotten, Nor the hope of the afflicted perish forever.

Ps. 31:24 - Be strong and let your heart take courage, All you who hope in the Lord.

Ps. 33:17 - A horse is a false hope for victory; Nor does it deliver anyone by its great strength.

Ps. 33:18 - Behold, the eye of the Lord is on those who fear Him, On those who hope for His lovingkindness.

Ps. 38:15 - For I hope in You, O Lord; You will answer, O Lord my God.

Ps. 39:7 - And now, Lord, for what do I wait? My hope is in You.

Ps. 42:5 - Why are you in despair, O my soul? And why have you become disturbed within me? Hope in God, for I shall again praise Him For the help of His presence.

Ps. 42:11 - Why are you in despair, O my soul? And why have you become disturbed within me? Hope in God, for I shall yet praise Him, The help of my countenance and my God.

Ps. 43:5 - Why are you in despair, O my soul? And why are you disturbed within me? Hope in God, for I shall again praise Him, The help of my countenance and my God.

Ps. 62:5 - My soul, wait in silence for God only, For my hope is from Him.

Ps. 62:10 - Do not trust in oppression And do not vainly hope in robbery; If riches increase, do not set your heart upon them.

Ps. 71:5 - For You are my hope; O Lord God, You are my confidence from my youth.

Ps. 71:14 - But as for me, I will hope continually, And will praise You yet more and more.

Ps. 119:49 - Remember the word to Your servant, In which You have made me hope.

Ps. 119:116 - Sustain me according to Your word, that I may live; And do not let me be ashamed of my hope.

Ps. 119:166 - I hope for Your salvation, O Lord, And do Your commandments.

Ps. 130:5 - I wait for the Lord, my soul does wait, And in His word do I hope.

Ps. 130:7 - O Israel, hope in the Lord; For with the Lord there is lovingkindness, And with Him is abundant redemption.

Ps. 131:3 - O Israel, hope in the Lord From this time forth and forever.

Ps. 146:5 - How blessed is he whose help is the God of Jacob, Whose hope is in the Lord his God.

HORN

Ps. 18:2 - The Lord is my rock and my fortress and my deliverer, My God, my rock, in whom I take refuge; My shield and the horn of my salvation, my stronghold.

Ps. 75:4 - I said to the boastful, "Do not boast," And to the wicked, "Do not lift up the horn."

Ps. 75:5 - Do not lift up your horn on high, Do not speak with insolent pride.

Ps. 89:17 - For You are the glory of their strength, And by Your favor our horn is exalted.

Ps. 89:24 - My faithfulness and My lovingkindness will be with him, And in My name his horn will be exalted.

Ps. 92:10 - But You have exalted my horn like that of the wild ox; I have been anointed with fresh oil.

Ps. 98:6 - With trumpets and the sound of the horn Shout joyfully before the King, the Lord.

Ps. 112:9 - He has given freely to the poor, His righteousness endures forever; His horn will be exalted in honor.

Ps. 132:17 - There I will cause the horn of David to spring forth; I have prepared a lamp for Mine anointed.

Ps. 148:14 - And He has lifted up a horn for His people, Praise for all His godly ones; Even for the sons of Israel, a people near to Him. Praise the Lord!

INHERITANCE

Ps. 2:8 -Ask of Me, and I will surely give the nations as Your inheritance, And the very ends of the earth as Your possession.

Ps. 16:5 - The Lord is the portion of my inheritance and my cup; You support my lot.

Ps. 28:9 - Save Your people and bless Your inheritance; Be their shepherd also, and carry them forever.

Ps. 33:12 - Blessed is the nation whose God is the Lord, The people whom He has chosen for His own inheritance.

Ps. 37:18 - The Lord knows the days of the blameless, And their inheritance will be forever.

Ps. 47:4 - He chooses our inheritance for us, The glory of Jacob whom He loves.

Ps. 61:5 - For You have heard my vows, O God; You have given me the inheritance of those who fear Your name.

Ps. 68:9 - You shed abroad a plentiful rain, O God; You confirmed Your inheritance when it was parched.

Ps. 74:2 - Remember Your congregation, which You have purchased of old, Which You have redeemed to be the tribe of Your inheritance; And this Mount Zion, where You have dwelt.

Ps. 78:55 - He also drove out the nations before them And apportioned them for an inheritance by measurement, And made the tribes of Israel dwell in their tents.

Ps. 78:62 - He also delivered His people to the sword, And was filled with wrath at His inheritance.

Ps. 78:71 - From the care of the ewes with suckling lambs He brought him To shepherd Jacob His people, And Israel His inheritance.

Ps. 79:1 - O God, the nations have invaded Your inheritance; They have defiled Your holy temple; They have laid Jerusalem in ruins.

Ps. 94:14 - For the Lord will not abandon His people, Nor will He forsake His inheritance.

Ps. 105:11 - Saying, "To you I will give the land of Canaan As the portion of your inheritance."

Ps. 106:5 - That I may see the prosperity of Your chosen ones, That I may rejoice in the gladness of Your nation, That I may glory with Your inheritance.

Ps. 106:40 - Therefore the anger of the Lord was kindled against His people And He abhorred His inheritance.

INTEGRITY

Ps. 7:8 - The Lord judges the peoples; Vindicate me, O Lord, according to my righteousness and my integrity that is in me.

Ps. 15:2 - He who walks with integrity, and works righteousness, And speaks truth in his heart.

Ps. 25:21 - Let integrity and uprightness preserve me, For I wait for You.

Ps. 26:1 - Vindicate me, O Lord, for I have walked in my integrity, And I have trusted in the Lord without wavering.

Ps. 26:11 - But as for me, I shall walk in my integrity; Redeem me, and be gracious to me.

Ps. 41:12 - As for me, You uphold me in my integrity, And You set me in Your presence forever.

Ps. 78:72 - So he shepherded them according to the integrity of his heart, And guided them with his skillful hands.

Ps. 101:2 - I will give heed to the blameless way. When will You come to me? I will walk within my house in the integrity of my heart.

JOY

Ps. 5:11 - But let all who take refuge in You be glad, Let them ever sing for joy; And may You shelter them, That those who love Your name may exult in You.

Ps. 16:11 - You will make known to me the path of life; In Your presence is fullness of joy; In Your right hand there are pleasures forever.

Ps. 20:5 - We will sing for joy over your victory, And in the name of our God we will set up our banners. May the Lord fulfill all your petitions.

Ps. 27:6 - And now my head will be lifted up above my enemies around me, And I will offer in His tent sacrifices with shouts of joy; I will sing, yes, I will sing praises to the Lord.

Ps. 30:5 - For His anger is but for a moment, His favor is for a lifetime; Weeping may last for the night, But a shout of joy comes in the morning.

Ps. 32:11 - Be glad in the Lord and rejoice, you righteous ones; And shout for joy, all you who are upright in heart.

Ps. 33:1 - Sing for joy in the Lord, O you righteous ones; Praise is becoming to the upright.

Ps. 33:3 - Sing to Him a new song; Play skillfully with a shout of joy.

Ps. 35:27 - Let them shout for joy and rejoice, who favor my vindication; And let them say continually, "The Lord be magnified, Who delights in the prosperity of His servant."

Ps. 42:4 - These things I remember and I pour out my soul within me. For I used to go along with the throng and lead them in procession to the house of God, With the voice of joy and thanksgiving, a multitude keeping festival.

Ps. 43:4 - Then I will go to the altar of God, To God my exceeding joy; And upon the lyre I shall praise You, O God, my God.

Ps. 45:7 - You have loved righteousness and hated wickedness; Therefore God, Your God, has anointed You With the oil of joy above Your fellows.

Ps. 47:1 - O clap your hands, all peoples; Shout to God with the voice of joy.

Ps. 48:2 - Beautiful in elevation, the joy of the whole earth, Is Mount Zion in the far north, The city of the great King.

Ps. 51:8 - Make me to hear joy and gladness, Let the bones which You have broken rejoice.

Ps. 51:12 - Restore to me the joy of Your salvation And sustain me with a willing spirit.

Ps. 63:7 - For You have been my help, And in the shadow of Your wings I sing for joy.

Ps. 65:8 - They who dwell in the ends of the earth stand in awe of Your signs; You make the dawn and the sunset shout for joy.

Ps. 65:13 - The meadows are clothed with flocks And the valleys are covered with grain; They shout for joy, yes, they sing.

Ps. 67:4 - Let the nations be glad and sing for joy; For You will judge the peoples with uprightness And guide the nations on the earth.

Ps. 71:23 - My lips will shout for joy when I sing praises to You; And my soul, which You have redeemed.

Ps. 81:1 - Sing for joy to God our strength; Shout joyfully to the God of Jacob.

Ps. 84:2 - My soul longed and even yearned for the courts of the Lord; My heart and my flesh sing for joy to the living God.

Ps. 87:7 - Then those who sing as well as those who play the flutes shall say, "All my springs of joy are in you."

Ps. 89:12 - The north and the south, You have created them; Tabor and Hermon shout for joy at Your name.

Ps. 90:14 - O satisfy us in the morning with Your lovingkindness, That we may sing for joy and be glad all our days.

Ps. 92:4 - For You, O Lord, have made me glad by what You have done, I will sing for joy at the works of Your hands.

Ps. 95:1 - O come, let us sing for joy to the Lord, Let us shout joyfully to the rock of our salvation.

Ps. 96:12 - Let the field exult, and all that is in it. Then all the trees of the forest will sing for joy.

Ps. 98:4 - Shout joyfully to the Lord, all the earth; Break forth and sing for joy and sing praises.

Ps. 98:8 - Let the rivers clap their hands, Let the mountains sing together for joy.

Ps. 105:43 - And He brought forth His people with joy, His chosen ones with a joyful shout.

Ps. 119:111 - I have inherited Your testimonies forever, For they are the joy of my heart.

Ps. 126:6 - He who goes to and fro weeping, carrying his bag of seed, Shall indeed come again with a shout of joy, bringing his sheaves with him.

Ps. 132:9 - Let Your priests be clothed with righteousness, And let Your godly ones sing for joy.

Ps. 132:16 - Her priests also I will clothe with salvation, And her godly ones will sing aloud for joy.

Ps. 137:6 - May my tongue cling to the roof of my mouth If I do not remember you, If I do not exalt Jerusalem Above my chief joy.

Ps. 149:5 - Let the godly ones exult in glory; Let them sing for joy on their beds.

JUSTICE

Ps. 25:9 - He leads the humble in justice, And He teaches the humble His way.

Ps. 33:5 - He loves righteousness and justice; The earth is full of the lovingkindness of the Lord.

Ps. 37:28 - For the Lord loves justice And does not forsake His godly ones; They are preserved forever, But the descendants of the wicked will be cut off.

Ps. 37:30 - The mouth of the righteous utters wisdom, And his tongue speaks justice.

Ps. 72:2 - May he judge Your people with righteousness And Your afflicted with justice.

Ps. 82:3 - Vindicate the weak and fatherless; Do justice to the afflicted and destitute.

Ps. 89:14 - Righteousness and justice are the foundation of Your throne; Lovingkindness and truth go before You.

Ps. 97:2 - Clouds and thick darkness surround Him; Righteousness and justice are the foundation of His throne.

Ps. 99:4 - The strength of the King loves justice; You have established equity; You have executed justice and righteousness in Jacob.

Ps. 101:1 - I will sing of lovingkindness and justice, To You, O Lord, I will sing praises.

Ps. 106:3 - How blessed are those who keep justice, Who practice righteousness at all times!

Ps. 111:7 - The works of His hands are truth and justice; All His precepts are sure.

Ps. 119:121 - I have done justice and righteousness; Do not leave me to my oppressors.

Ps. 140:12 - I know that the Lord will maintain the cause of the afflicted And justice for the poor.

Ps. 146:7 - Who executes justice for the oppressed; Who gives food to the hungry. The Lord sets the prisoners free.

KINGDOM

Ps. 22:28 - For the kingdom is the Lord's And He rules over the nations.

Ps. 45:6 - Your throne, O God, is forever and ever; A scepter of uprightness is the scepter of Your kingdom.

Ps. 105:13 - And they wandered about from nation to nation, From one kingdom to another people.

Ps. 145:11 - They shall speak of the glory of Your kingdom And talk of Your power.

Ps. 145:12 - To make known to the sons of men Your mighty acts And the glory of the majesty of Your kingdom.

Ps. 145:13 - Your kingdom is an everlasting kingdom, And Your dominion endures throughout all generations.

LAMP

Ps. 18:28 - For You light my lamp; The Lord my God illumines my darkness.

Ps. 119:105 - Your word is a lamp to my feet And a light to my path.

Ps. 132:17 - There I will cause the horn of David to spring forth; I have prepared a lamp for Mine anointed.

LAW

Ps. 1:2 - But his delight is in the law of the Lord, And in His law he meditates day and night.

Ps. 19:7 - The law of the Lord is perfect, restoring the soul; The testimony of the Lord is sure, making wise the simple.

Ps. 37:31 - The law of his God is in his heart; His steps do not slip.

Ps. 40:8 - I delight to do Your will, O my God; Your Law is within my heart.

Ps. 78:5 - For He established a testimony in Jacob And appointed a law in Israel, Which He commanded our fathers That they should teach them to their children.

Ps. 78:10 - They did not keep the covenant of God And refused to walk in His law.

Ps. 89:30 - If his sons forsake My law And do not walk in My judgments.

Ps. 94:12 - Blessed is the man whom You chasten, O Lord, And whom You teach out of Your law.

Ps. 119:1 - How blessed are those whose way is blameless, Who walk in the law of the Lord.

Ps. 119:18 - Open my eyes, that I may behold Wonderful things from Your law.

Ps. 119:29 - Remove the false way from me, And graciously grant me Your law.

Ps. 119:34 - Give me understanding, that I may observe Your law And keep it with all my heart.

Ps. 119:44 - So I will keep Your law continually, Forever and ever.

Ps. 119:51 - The arrogant utterly deride me, Yet I do not turn aside from Your law.

Ps. 119:53 - Burning indignation has seized me because of the wicked, Who forsake Your law.

Ps. 119:55 - O Lord, I remember Your name in the night, And keep Your law.

Ps. 119:61 - The cords of the wicked have encircled me, But I have not forgotten Your law.

Ps. 119:70 - Their heart is covered with fat, But I delight in Your law.

Ps. 119:72 - The law of Your mouth is better to me Than thousands of gold and silver pieces.

Ps. 119:77 - May Your compassion come to me that I may live, For Your law is my delight.

Ps. 119:85 - The arrogant have dug pits for me, Men who are not in accord with Your law.

Ps. 119:92 - If Your law had not been my delight, Then I would have perished in my affliction.

Ps. 119:97 - O how I love Your law! It is my meditation all the day.

Ps. 119:109 - My life is continually in my hand, Yet I do not forget Your law.

Ps. 119:113 - I hate those who are double-minded, But I love Your law.

Ps. 119:126 - It is time for the Lord to act, For they have broken Your law.

Ps. 119:136 - My eyes shed streams of water, Because they do not keep Your law.

Ps. 119:142 - Your righteousness is an everlasting righteousness, And Your law is truth.

Ps. 119:150 - Those who follow after wickedness draw near; They are far from Your law.

Ps. 119:153 - Look upon my affliction and rescue me, For I do not forget Your law.

Ps. 119:163 - I hate and despise falsehood, But I love Your law.

Ps. 119:165 - Those who love Your law have great peace, And nothing causes them to stumble.

Ps. 119:174 - I long for Your salvation, O Lord, And Your law is my delight.

LISTEN

Ps. 34:11 - Come, you children, listen to me; I will teach you the fear of the Lord.

Ps. 45:10 - Listen, O daughter, give attention and incline your ear: Forget your people and your father's house.

Ps. 78:1 - Listen, O my people, to my instruction; Incline your ears to the words of my mouth.

Ps. 81:8 - Hear, O My people, and I will admonish you; O Israel, if you would listen to Me!

Ps. 81:11 - But My people did not listen to My voice, And Israel did not obey Me.

Ps. 81:13 - Oh that My people would listen to Me, That Israel would walk in My ways!

Ps. 106:25 - But grumbled in their tents; They did not listen to the voice of the Lord.

LIVE

Ps. 22:26 - The afflicted will eat and be satisfied; Those who seek Him will praise the Lord. Let your heart live forever!

Ps. 49:9 - That he should live on eternally, That he should not undergo decay.

Ps. 55:23 - But You, O God, will bring them down to the pit of destruction; Men of bloodshed and deceit will not live out half their days. But I will trust in You.

Ps. 63:4 - So I will bless You as long as I live; I will lift up my hands in Your name.

Ps. 72:15 - So may he live, and may the gold of Sheba be given to him; And let them pray for him continually; Let them bless him all day long.

Ps. 89:48 - What man can live and not see death? Can he deliver his soul from the power of Sheol?

Ps. 104:33 - I will sing to the Lord as long as I live; I will sing praise to my God while I have my being.

Ps. 116:2 - Because He has inclined His ear to me, Therefore I shall call upon Him as long as I live.

Ps. 118:17 - I will not die, but live, And tell of the works of the Lord.

Ps. 119:17 - Deal bountifully with Your servant, That I may live and keep Your word.

Ps. 119:77 - May Your compassion come to me that I may live, For Your law is my delight.

Ps. 119:116 - Sustain me according to Your word, that I may live; And do not let me be ashamed of my hope.

Ps. 119:144 - Your testimonies are righteous forever; Give me understanding that I may live.

Ps. 119:175 - Let my soul live that it may praise You, And let Your ordinances help me.

Ps. 146:2 - I will praise the Lord while I live; I will sing praises to my God while I have my being.

LOVE

Ps. 4:2 - O sons of men, how long will my honor become a reproach? How long will you love what is worthless and aim at deception?

Ps. 5:11 - But let all who take refuge in You be glad, Let them ever sing for joy; And may You shelter them, That those who love Your name may exult in You.

Ps.18:1 - I love You, O Lord, my strength.

Ps. 26:8 - O Lord, I love the habitation of Your house And the place where Your glory dwells.

Ps. 31:23 - O love the Lord, all you His godly ones! The Lord preserves the faithful And fully recompenses the proud doer.

Ps. 40:16 - Let all who seek You rejoice and be glad in You; Let those who love Your salvation say continually, "The Lord be magnified!"

Ps. 45:1 - My heart overflows with a good theme; I address my verses to the King; My tongue is the pen of a ready writer.

Ps. 52:3 - You love evil more than good, Falsehood more than speaking what is right.

Ps. 52:4 - You love all words that devour, O deceitful tongue.

Ps. 69:36 - The descendants of His servants will inherit it, And those who love His name will dwell in it.

Ps. 70:4 - Let all who seek You rejoice and be glad in You; And let those who love Your salvation say continually, "Let God be magnified."

Ps. 97:10 - Hate evil, you who love the Lord, Who preserves the souls of His godly ones; He delivers them from the hand of the wicked.

Ps. 109:4 - In return for my love they act as my accusers; But I am in prayer.

Ps. 109:5 - Thus they have repaid me evil for good And hatred for my love.

Ps. 116:1 - I love the Lord, because He hears My voice and my supplications.

Ps. 119:47 - I shall delight in Your commandments, Which I love.

Ps. 119:48 - And I shall lift up my hands to Your commandments, Which I love; And I will meditate on Your statutes.

Ps. 119:97 - O how I love Your law! It is my meditation all the day.

Ps. 119:113 - I hate those who are double-minded, But I love Your law.

Ps. 119:119 - You have removed all the wicked of the earth like dross; Therefore I love Your testimonies.

Ps. 119:127 - Therefore I love Your commandments Above gold, yes, above fine gold.

Ps. 119:132 - Turn to me and be gracious to me, After Your manner with those who love Your name.

Ps. 119:159 - Consider how I love Your precepts; Revive me, O Lord, according to Your lovingkindness.

Ps. 119:163 - I hate and despise falsehood, But I love Your law.

Ps. 119:165 - Those who love Your law have great peace, And nothing causes them to stumble.

Ps. 119:167 - My soul keeps Your testimonies, And I love them exceedingly.

Ps. 122:6 - Pray for the peace of Jerusalem: May they prosper who love you.

Ps. 145:20 - The Lord keeps all who love Him, But all the wicked He will destroy.

MAJESTIC

Ps. 8:1 - O Lord, our Lord, How majestic is Your name in all the earth, Who have displayed Your splendor above the heavens!

Ps. 8:9 - O Lord, our Lord, How majestic is Your name in all the earth!

Ps. 16:3 - As for the saints who are in the earth, They are the majestic ones in whom is all my delight.

Ps. 29:4 - The voice of the Lord is powerful, The voice of the Lord is majestic.

Ps. 76:4 - You are resplendent, More majestic than the mountains of prey.

Ps. 111:3 - Splendid and majestic is His work, And His righteousness endures forever.

Chapter Two

MARVELOUS

Ps. 31:21 - Blessed be the Lord, For He has made marvelous His lovingkindness to me in a besieged city.
Ps. 118:23 - This is the Lord's doing; It is marvelous in our eyes.

MEDITATE

Ps. 4:4 - Tremble, and do not sin; Meditate in your heart upon your bed, and be still.
Ps. 27:4 - One thing I have asked from the Lord, that I shall seek: That I may dwell in the house of the Lord all the days of my life, To behold the beauty of the Lord And to meditate in His temple.
Ps. 63:6 - When I remember You on my bed, I meditate on You in the night watches.
Ps. 77:6 - I will remember my song in the night; I will meditate with my heart, And my spirit ponders.
Ps. 77:12 - I will meditate on all Your work And muse on Your deeds.
Ps. 119:15 - I will meditate on Your precepts And regard Your ways.
Ps. 119:27 - Make me understand the way of Your precepts, So I will meditate on Your wonders.
Ps. 119:48 - And I shall lift up my hands to Your commandments, Which I love; And I will meditate on Your statutes.
Ps. 119:78 - May the arrogant be ashamed, for they subvert me with a lie; But I shall meditate on Your precepts.
Ps. 119:148 - My eyes anticipate the night watches, That I may meditate on Your word.
Ps. 143:5 - I remember the days of old; I meditate on all Your doings; I muse on the work of Your hands.

Ps. 145:5 - On the glorious splendor of Your majesty And on Your wonderful works, I will meditate.

MIGHTY

Ps. 10:10 - He crouches, he bows down, And the unfortunate fall by his mighty ones.

Ps. 18:17 - He delivered me from my strong enemy, And from those who hated me, for they were too mighty for me.

Ps. 24:8 - Who is the King of glory? The Lord strong and mighty, The Lord mighty in battle.

Ps. 29:1 - Ascribe to the Lord, O sons of the mighty, Ascribe to the Lord glory and strength.

Ps. 33:16 - The king is not saved by a mighty army; A warrior is not delivered by great strength.

Ps. 35:18 - I will give You thanks in the great congregation; I will praise You among a mighty throng.

Ps. 45:3 - Gird Your sword on Your thigh, O Mighty One, In Your splendor and Your majesty!

Ps. 50:1 - The Mighty One, God, the Lord, has spoken, And summoned the earth from the rising of the sun to its setting.

Ps. 52:1 - Why do you boast in evil, O mighty man? The lovingkindness of God endures all day long.

Ps. 68:33 - To Him who rides upon the highest heavens, which are from ancient times; Behold, He speaks forth with His voice, a mighty voice.

Ps. 71:16 - I will come with the mighty deeds of the Lord God; I will make mention of Your righteousness, Yours alone.

Ps. 77:19 - Your way was in the sea And Your paths in the mighty waters, And Your footprints may not be known.

Ps. 89:6 - For who in the skies is comparable to the Lord? Who among the sons of the mighty is like the Lord.

Ps. 89:8 - O Lord God of hosts, who is like You, O mighty Lord? Your faithfulness also surrounds You.

Ps. 89:10 - You Yourself crushed Rahab like one who is slain; You scattered Your enemies with Your mighty arm.

Ps. 89:13 - You have a strong arm; Your hand is mighty, Your right hand is exalted.

Ps. 89:19 - Once You spoke in vision to Your godly ones, And said, "I have given help to one who is mighty; I have exalted one chosen from the people."

Ps. 93:4 - More than the sounds of many waters, Than the mighty breakers of the sea, The Lord on high is mighty.

Ps. 103:20 - Bless the Lord, you His angels, Mighty in strength, who perform His word, Obeying the voice of His word!

Ps. 106:2 - Who can speak of the mighty deeds of the Lord, Or can show forth all His praise?

Ps. 112:2 - His descendants will be mighty on earth; The generation of the upright will be blessed.

Ps. 132:2 - How he swore to the Lord And vowed to the Mighty One of Jacob.

Ps. 132:5 - Until I find a place for the Lord, A dwelling place for the Mighty One of Jacob.

Ps. 135:10 - He smote many nations And slew mighty kings.

Ps. 136:18 - And slew mighty kings, For His lovingkindness is everlasting.

Ps. 145:4 - One generation shall praise Your works to another, And shall declare Your mighty acts.

Ps. 145:12 - To make known to the sons of men Your mighty acts And the glory of the majesty of Your kingdom.

Ps. 150:1 - Praise the Lord! Praise God in His sanctuary; Praise Him in His mighty expanse.

Ps. 150:2 - Praise Him for His mighty deeds; Praise Him according to His excellent greatness.

OIL

Ps. 23:5 - You prepare a table before me in the presence of my enemies; You have anointed my head with oil; My cup overflows.

Ps. 45:7 - You have loved righteousness and hated wickedness; Therefore God, Your God, has anointed You With the oil of joy above Your fellows.

Ps. 55:21 - His speech was smoother than butter, But his heart was war; His words were softer than oil, Yet they were drawn swords.

Ps. 89:20 - I have found David My servant; With My holy oil I have anointed him.

Ps. 92:10 - But You have exalted my horn like that of the wild ox; I have been anointed with fresh oil.

Ps. 104:15 - And wine which makes man's heart glad, So that he may make his face glisten with oil, And food which sustains man's heart.

Ps. 109:18 - But he clothed himself with cursing as with his garment, And it entered into his body like water And like oil into his bones.

Ps. 133:2 - It is like the precious oil upon the head, Coming down upon the beard, Even Aaron's beard, Coming down upon the edge of his robes.

Ps. 141:5 - Let the righteous smite me in kindness and reprove me; It is oil upon the head; Do not let my head refuse it, For still my prayer is against their wicked deeds.

PASTURE

Ps. 74:1 - O God, why have You rejected us forever? Why does Your anger smoke against the sheep of Your pasture?

Ps. 79:13 - So we Your people and the sheep of Your pasture Will give thanks to You forever; To all generations we will tell of Your praise.

Ps. 95:7 - For He is our God, And we are the people of His pasture and the sheep of His hand. Today, if you would hear His voice.

Ps. 100:3 - Know that the Lord Himself is God; It is He who has made us, and not we ourselves; We are His people and the sheep of His pasture.

PEACE

Ps. 4:8 - In peace I will both lie down and sleep, For You alone, O Lord, make me to dwell in safety.

Ps. 28:3 - Do not drag me away with the wicked And with those who work iniquity, Who speak peace with their neighbors, While evil is in their hearts.

Ps. 29:11 - The Lord will give strength to His people; The Lord will bless His people with peace.

Ps. 34:14 - Depart from evil and do good; Seek peace and pursue it.

Ps. 35:20 - For they do not speak peace, But they devise deceitful words against those who are quiet in the land.

Ps. 37:37 - Mark the blameless man, and behold the upright; For the man of peace will have a posterity.

Ps. 55:18 - He will redeem my soul in peace from the battle which is against me, For they are many who strive with me.

Ps. 55:20 - He has put forth his hands against those who were at peace with him; He has violated his covenant.

Ps. 69:22 - May their table before them become a snare; And when they are in peace, may it become a trap.

Ps. 72:3 - Let the mountains bring peace to the people, And the hills, in righteousness.

Ps. 72:7 - In his days may the righteous flourish, And abundance of peace till the moon is no more.

Ps. 85:8 - I will hear what God the Lord will say; For He will speak peace to His people, to His godly ones; But let them not turn back to folly.

Ps. 85:10 - Lovingkindness and truth have met together; Righteousness and peace have kissed each other.

Ps. 119:165 - Those who love Your law have great peace, And nothing causes them to stumble.

Ps. 120:6 - Too long has my soul had its dwelling With those who hate peace.

Ps. 120:7 - I am for peace, but when I speak, They are for war.

Ps. 122:6 - Pray for the peace of Jerusalem: "May they prosper who love you.

Ps. 122:7 - May peace be within your walls, And prosperity within your palaces.

Ps. 122:8 - For the sake of my brothers and my friends, I will now say, "May peace be within you."

Ps. 125:5 - But as for those who turn aside to their crooked ways, The Lord will lead them away with the doers of iniquity. Peace be upon Israel.

Ps. 128:6 - Indeed, may you see your children's children. Peace be upon Israel!

Ps. 147:14 - He makes peace in your borders; He satisfies you with the finest of the wheat.

POWER
Ps. 21:13 - Be exalted, O Lord, in Your strength; We will sing and praise Your power.

Ps. 22:20 - Deliver my soul from the sword, My only life from the power of the dog.

Ps. 49:15 - But God will redeem my soul from the power of Sheol, For He will receive me.

Ps. 54:1 - A Maskil of David, when the Ziphites came and said to Saul, "Is not David hiding himself among us?" Save me, O God, by Your name, And vindicate me by Your power.

Ps. 59:11 - Do not slay them, or my people will forget; Scatter them by Your power, and bring them down, O Lord, our shield.

Ps. 62:11 - Once God has spoken; Twice I have heard this: That power belongs to God.

Ps. 63:2 - Thus I have seen You in the sanctuary, To see Your power and Your glory.

Ps. 63:10 - They will be delivered over to the power of the sword; They will be a prey for foxes.

Ps. 66:3 - Say to God, "How awesome are Your works! Because of the greatness of Your power Your enemies will give feigned obedience to You."

Ps. 68:35 - O God, You are awesome from Your sanctuary. The God of Israel Himself gives strength and power to the people. Blessed be God!

Ps. 71:18 - And even when I am old and gray, O God, do not forsake me, Until I declare Your strength to this generation, Your power to all who are to come.

Ps. 77:15 - You have by Your power redeemed Your people, The sons of Jacob and Joseph.

Ps. 78:26 - He caused the east wind to blow in the heavens And by His power He directed the south wind.

Ps. 78:42 - They did not remember His power, The day when He redeemed them from the adversary.

Ps. 79:11 - Let the groaning of the prisoner come before You; According to the greatness of Your power preserve those who are doomed to die.

Ps. 80:2 - Before Ephraim and Benjamin and Manasseh, stir up Your power And come to save us!

Ps. 89:48 - What man can live and not see death? Can he deliver his soul from the power of Sheol?

Ps. 90:11 - Who understands the power of Your anger And Your fury, according to the fear that is due You?

Ps. 106:8 - Nevertheless He saved them for the sake of His name, That He might make His power known.

Ps. 106:42 - Their enemies also oppressed them, And they were subdued under their power.

Ps. 110:3 - Your people will volunteer freely in the day of Your power; In holy array, from the womb of the dawn, Your youth are to You as the dew.

Ps. 111:6 - He has made known to His people the power of His works, In giving them the heritage of the nations.

Ps. 145:6 - Men shall speak of the power of Your awesome acts, And I will tell of Your greatness.

Ps. 145:11 - They shall speak of the glory of Your kingdom And talk of Your power.

PRAISE

Ps. 7:17 - I will give thanks to the Lord according to His righteousness And will sing praise to the name of the Lord Most High.

Ps. 9:2 - I will be glad and exult in You; I will sing praise to Your name, O Most High.

Ps. 21:13 - Be exalted, O Lord, in Your strength; We will sing and praise Your power.

Ps. 22:22 - I will tell of Your name to my brethren; In the midst of the assembly I will praise You.

Ps. 22:23 - You who fear the Lord, praise Him; All you descendants of Jacob, glorify Him, And stand in awe of Him, all you descendants of Israel.

Ps. 22:25 - From You comes my praise in the great assembly; I shall pay my vows before those who fear Him.

Ps. 22:26 - The afflicted will eat and be satisfied; Those who seek Him will praise the Lord. Let your heart live forever!

Ps. 30:4 - Sing praise to the Lord, you His godly ones, And give thanks to His holy name.

Ps. 30:9 - What profit is there in my blood, if I go down to the pit? Will the dust praise You? Will it declare Your faithfulness?

Ps. 30:12 - That my soul may sing praise to You and not be silent. O Lord my God, I will give thanks to You forever.

Ps. 33:1 - Sing for joy in the Lord, O you righteous ones; Praise is becoming to the upright.

Ps. 34:1 - A Psalm of David when he feigned madness before Abimelech, who drove him away and he departed. I will bless the Lord at all times; His praise shall continually be in my mouth.

Ps. 35:18 - I will give You thanks in the great congregation; I will praise You among a mighty throng.

Ps. 35:28 - And my tongue shall declare Your righteousness And Your praise all day long.

Ps. 40:3 - He put a new song in my mouth, a song of praise to our God; Many will see and fear And will trust in the Lord.

Ps. 42:5 - Why are you in despair, O my soul? And why have you become disturbed within me? Hope in God, for I shall again praise Him For the help of His presence.

Ps. 42:11 - Why are you in despair, O my soul? And why have you become disturbed within me? Hope in God, for I shall yet praise Him, The help of my countenance and my God.

Ps. 43:4 - Then I will go to the altar of God, To God my exceeding joy; And upon the lyre I shall praise You, O God, my God.

Ps. 43:5 - Why are you in despair, O my soul? And why are you disturbed within me? Hope in God, for I shall again praise Him, The help of my countenance and my God.

Ps. 48:10 - As is Your name, O God, So is Your praise to the ends of the earth; Your right hand is full of righteousness.

Ps. 49:18 - Though while he lives he congratulates himself— And though men praise you when you do well for yourself.

Ps. 51:15 - O Lord, open my lips, That my mouth may declare Your praise.

Ps. 56:4 - In God, whose word I praise, In God I have put my trust; I shall not be afraid. What can mere man do to me?

Ps. 56:10 - In God, whose word I praise, In the Lord, whose word I praise.

Ps. 61:8 - So I will sing praise to Your name forever, That I may pay my vows day by day.

Ps. 63:3 - Because Your lovingkindness is better than life, My lips will praise You.

Ps. 65:1 - There will be silence before You, and praise in Zion, O God, And to You the vow will be performed.

Ps. 66:2 - Sing the glory of His name; Make His praise glorious.

Ps. 66:8 - Bless our God, O peoples, And sound His praise abroad.

Ps. 67:3 - Let the peoples praise You, O God; Let all the peoples praise You.

Ps. 67:5 - Let the peoples praise You, O God; Let all the peoples praise You.

Ps. 69:30 - I will praise the name of God with song And magnify Him with thanksgiving.

Ps. 69:34 - Let heaven and earth praise Him, The seas and everything that moves in them.

Ps. 71:6 - By You I have been sustained from my birth; You are He who took me from my mother's womb; My praise is continually of You.

Ps. 71:8 - My mouth is filled with Your praise And with Your glory all day long.

Ps. 71:14 - But as for me, I will hope continually, And will praise You yet more and more.

Ps. 71:22 - I will also praise You with a harp, Even Your truth, O my God; To You I will sing praises with the lyre, O Holy One of Israel.

Ps. 74:21 - Let not the oppressed return dishonored; Let the afflicted and needy praise Your name.

Ps. 76:10 - For the wrath of man shall praise You; With a remnant of wrath You will gird Yourself.

Ps. 79:13 - So we Your people and the sheep of Your pasture Will give thanks to You forever; To all generations we will tell of Your praise.

Ps. 88:10 - Will You perform wonders for the dead? Will the departed spirits rise and praise You?

Ps. 89:5 - The heavens will praise Your wonders, O Lord; Your faithfulness also in the assembly of the holy ones.

Ps. 99:3 - Let them praise Your great and awesome name; Holy is He.

Ps. 100:4 - Enter His gates with thanksgiving And His courts with praise. Give thanks to Him, bless His name.

Ps. 102:18 - This will be written for the generation to come, That a people yet to be created may praise the Lord.

Ps. 102:21 - That men may tell of the name of the Lord in Zion And His praise in Jerusalem.

Ps. 104:33 - I will sing to the Lord as long as I live; I will sing praise to my God while I have my being.

Ps. 104:35 - Let sinners be consumed from the earth And let the wicked be no more. Bless the Lord, O my soul. Praise the Lord!

Ps. 105:45 - So that they might keep His statutes And observe His laws, Praise the Lord!

Ps. 106:1 - Praise the Lord! Oh give thanks to the Lord, for He is good; For His lovingkindness is everlasting.

Ps. 106:2 - Who can speak of the mighty deeds of the Lord, Or can show forth all His praise?

Ps. 106:12 - Then they believed His words; They sang His praise.

Ps. 106:47 - Save us, O Lord our God, And gather us from among the nations, To give thanks to Your holy name And glory in Your praise.

Ps. 106:48 - Blessed be the Lord, the God of Israel, From everlasting even to everlasting. And let all the people say, "Amen." Praise the Lord!

Ps. 107:32 - Let them extol Him also in the congregation of the people, And praise Him at the seat of the elders.

Ps. 109:1 - O God of my praise, Do not be silent!

Ps. 109:30 - With my mouth I will give thanks abundantly to the Lord; And in the midst of many I will praise Him.

Ps. 111:1 - Praise the Lord! I will give thanks to the Lord with all my heart, In the company of the upright and in the assembly.

Ps. 111:10 - The fear of the Lord is the beginning of wisdom; A good understanding have all those who do His commandments; His praise endures forever.

Ps. 112:1 - Praise the Lord! How blessed is the man who fears the Lord, Who greatly delights in His commandments.

Ps. 113:1 - Praise the Lord! Praise, O servants of the Lord, Praise the name of the Lord.

Ps. 113:9 - He makes the barren woman abide in the house As a joyful mother of children. Praise the Lord!

Ps. 115:17 - The dead do not praise the Lord, Nor do any who go down into silence.

Ps. 115:18 - But as for us, we will bless the Lord From this time forth and forever. Praise the Lord!

Ps. 116:19 - In the courts of the Lord's house, In the midst of you, O Jerusalem. Praise the Lord!

Ps. 117:1 - Praise the Lord, all nations; Laud Him, all peoples!

Ps. 117:2 - For His lovingkindness is great toward us, And the truth of the Lord is everlasting. Praise the Lord!

Ps. 119:164 - Seven times a day I praise You, Because of Your righteous ordinances.

Ps. 119:171 - Let my lips utter praise, For You teach me Your statutes.

Ps. 119:175 - Let my soul live that it may praise You, And let Your ordinances help me.

Ps. 135:1 - Praise the Lord! Praise the name of the Lord; Praise Him, O servants of the Lord.

Ps. 135:3 - Praise the Lord, for the Lord is good; Sing praises to His name, for it is lovely.

Ps. 135:21 - Blessed be the Lord from Zion, Who dwells in Jerusalem. Praise the Lord!

Ps. 145:1 - I will extol You, my God, O King, And I will bless Your name forever and ever.

Ps. 145:2 - Every day I will bless You, And I will praise Your name forever and ever.

Ps. 145:4 - One generation shall praise Your works to another, And shall declare Your mighty acts.

Ps. 145:21 - My mouth will speak the praise of the Lord, And all flesh will bless His holy name forever and ever.

Ps. 146:1 - Praise the Lord! Praise the Lord, O my soul!

Ps. 146:2 - I will praise the Lord while I live; I will sing praises to my God while I have my being.

Ps. 146:10 - The Lord will reign forever, Your God, O Zion, to all generations. Praise the Lord!

Ps. 147:1 - Praise the Lord! For it is good to sing praises to our God; For it is pleasant and praise is becoming.

Ps. 147:12 - Praise the Lord, O Jerusalem! Praise your God, O Zion!

Ps. 147:20 - He has not dealt thus with any nation; And as for His ordinances, they have not known them. Praise the Lord!

Ps. 148:1 - Praise the Lord! Praise the Lord from the heavens; Praise Him in the heights!

Ps. 148:2 - Praise Him, all His angels; Praise Him, all His hosts!

Ps. 148:3 - Praise Him, sun and moon; Praise Him, all stars of light!

Ps. 148:4 - Praise Him, highest heavens, And the waters that are above the heavens!

Ps. 148:5 - Let them praise the name of the Lord, For He commanded and they were created.

Ps. 148:7 - Praise the Lord from the earth, Sea monsters and all deeps.

Ps. 148:13 - Let them praise the name of the Lord, For His name alone is exalted; His glory is above earth and heaven.

Ps. 148:14 - And He has lifted up a horn for His people, Praise for all His godly ones; Even for the sons of Israel, a people near to Him. Praise the Lord!

Ps. 149:1 - Praise the Lord! Sing to the Lord a new song, And His praise in the congregation of the godly ones.

Ps. 149:3 - Let them praise His name with dancing; Let them sing praises to Him with timbrel and lyre.

Ps. 149:9 - To execute on them the judgment written; This is an honor for all His godly ones. Praise the Lord!

Ps. 150:1 - Praise the Lord! Praise God in His sanctuary; Praise Him in His mighty expanse.

Ps. 150:2 - Praise Him for His mighty deeds; Praise Him according to His excellent greatness.

Ps. 150:3 - Praise Him with trumpet sound; Praise Him with harp and lyre.

Ps. 150:4 - Praise Him with timbrel and dancing; Praise Him with stringed instruments and pipe.

Ps. 150:5 - Praise Him with loud cymbals; Praise Him with resounding cymbals.

Ps. 150:6 - Let everything that has breath praise the Lord. Praise the Lord!

PRAY

Ps. 5:2 - Give heed to the voice of my cry, My King and my God, For to You I will pray.[3]

Ps. 32:6 - For this cause everyone who is godly shall pray to You In a time when You may be found; Surely in a flood of great waters They shall not come near him.

Ps. 55:17 - Evening and morning and at noon I will pray, and cry aloud, And He shall hear my voice.

---

[3] From this point forward all Scripture quotations are from the *New King James Version.*

Ps. 118:25 - Save now, I pray, O Lord; O Lord, I pray, send now prosperity.

Ps. 119:76 - Let, I pray, Your merciful kindness be for my comfort, According to Your word to Your servant.

Ps. 119:108 - Accept, I pray, the freewill offerings of my mouth, O Lord, And teach me Your judgments.

Ps. 122:6 - Pray for the peace of Jerusalem: May they prosper who love you.

PRESERVE

Ps. 12:7 - You shall keep them, O Lord, You shall preserve them from this generation forever.

Ps. 16:1 - Preserve me, O God, for in You I put my trust.

Ps. 25:21 - Let integrity and uprightness preserve me, For I wait for You.

Ps. 32:7 - You are my hiding place; You shall preserve me from trouble; You shall surround me with songs of deliverance.

Ps. 36:6 - Your righteousness is like the great mountains; Your judgments are a great deep; O Lord, You preserve man and beast.

Ps. 40:11 - Do not withhold Your tender mercies from me, O Lord; Let Your lovingkindness and Your truth continually preserve me.

Ps. 41:2 - The Lord will preserve him and keep him alive, And he will be blessed on the earth; You will not deliver him to the will of his enemies.

Ps. 61:7 - He shall abide before God forever. Oh, prepare mercy and truth, which may preserve him!

Ps. 64:1 - Hear my voice, O God, in my meditation; Preserve my life from fear of the enemy.

Ps. 79:11 - Let the groaning of the prisoner come before You; According to the greatness of Your power Preserve those who are appointed to die.

Ps. 86:2 - Preserve my life, for I am holy; You are my God; Save Your servant who trusts in You!

Ps. 121:7 - The Lord shall preserve you from all evil; He shall preserve your soul.

Ps. 121:8 - The Lord shall preserve your going out and your coming in From this time forth, and even forevermore.

Ps. 140:1 - Deliver me, O Lord, from evil men; Preserve me from violent men.

Ps. 140:4 - Keep me, O Lord, from the hands of the wicked; Preserve me from violent men, Who have purposed to make my steps stumble.

REDEEM

Ps. 25:22 - Redeem Israel, O God, Out of all their troubles!

Ps. 26:11 - But as for me, I will walk in my integrity; Redeem me and be merciful to me.

Ps. 44:26 - Arise for our help, And redeem us for Your mercies' sake.

Ps. 49:7 - None of them can by any means redeem his brother, Nor give to God a ransom for him.

Ps. 49:15 - But God will redeem my soul from the power of the grave, For He shall receive me.

Ps. 69:18 - Draw near to my soul, and redeem it; Deliver me because of my enemies.

Ps. 72:14 - He will redeem their life from oppression and violence; And precious shall be their blood in His sight.

Ps. 119:134 - Redeem me from the oppression of man, That I may keep Your precepts.

Ps. 119:154 - Plead my cause and redeem me; Revive me according to Your word.

Ps. 130:8 - And He shall redeem Israel From all his iniquities.

REFUGE

Ps. 9:9 - The Lord also will be a refuge for the oppressed, A refuge in times of trouble.

Ps. 14:6 - You shame the counsel of the poor, But the Lord is his refuge.

Ps. 28:8 - The Lord is their strength, And He is the saving refuge of His anointed.

Ps. 31:2 - Bow down Your ear to me, Deliver me speedily; Be my rock of refuge, A fortress of defense to save me.

Ps. 46:1 - God is our refuge and strength, A very present help in trouble.

Ps. 46:7 - The Lord of hosts is with us; The God of Jacob is our refuge.

Ps. 46:11 - The Lord of hosts is with us; The God of Jacob is our refuge.

Ps. 48:3 - God is in her palaces; He is known as her refuge.

Ps. 57:1 - Set to "Do Not Destroy." A Michtam of David when he fled from Saul into the cave. Be merciful to me, O God, be merciful to me! For my soul trusts in You; And in the shadow of Your wings I will make my refuge, Until these calamities have passed by.

Ps. 59:16 - But I will sing of Your power; Yes, I will sing aloud of Your mercy in the morning; For You have been my defense And refuge in the day of my trouble.

Ps. 62:7 - In God is my salvation and my glory; The rock of my strength, And my refuge, is in God.

Ps. 62:8 - Trust in Him at all times, you people; Pour out your heart before Him; God is a refuge for us.

Ps. 71:3 - Be my strong refuge, To which I may resort continually; You have given the commandment to save me, For You are my rock and my fortress.

Ps. 71:7 - I have become as a wonder to many, But You are my strong refuge.

Ps. 91:2 - I will say of the Lord, "He is my refuge and my fortress; My God, in Him I will trust."

Ps. 91:4 - He shall cover you with His feathers, And under His wings you shall take refuge; His truth shall be your shield and buckler.

Ps. 91:9 - Because you have made the Lord, who is my refuge, Even the Most High, your dwelling place.

Ps. 94:22 - But the Lord has been my defense, And my God the rock of my refuge.

Ps. 104:18 - The high hills are for the wild goats; The cliffs are a refuge for the rock badgers.

Ps. 141:8 - But my eyes are upon You, O God the Lord; In You I take refuge; Do not leave my soul destitute.

Ps. 142:4 - Look on my right hand and see, For there is no one who acknowledges me; Refuge has failed me; No one cares for my soul.

Ps. 142:5 - I cried out to You, O Lord: I said, "You are my refuge, My portion in the land of the living."

Ps. 144:2 - My lovingkindness and my fortress, My high tower and my deliverer, My shield and the One in whom I take refuge, Who subdues my people under me.

REJOICE
Ps. 2:11 - Serve the Lord with fear, And rejoice with trembling.

Ps. 5:11 - But let all those rejoice who put their trust in You; Let them ever shout for joy, because You defend them; Let those also who love Your name Be joyful in You.

Ps. 9:2 - I will be glad and rejoice in You; I will sing praise to Your name, O Most High.

Ps. 9:14 - That I may tell of all Your praise In the gates of the daughter of Zion. I will rejoice in Your salvation.

Ps. 13:4 - Lest my enemy say, "I have prevailed against him"; Lest those who trouble me rejoice when I am moved.

Ps. 13:5 - But I have trusted in Your mercy; My heart shall rejoice in Your salvation.

Ps. 14:7 - Oh, that the salvation of Israel would come out of Zion! When the Lord brings back the captivity of His people, Let Jacob rejoice and Israel be glad.

Ps. 20:5 - We will rejoice in your salvation, And in the name of our God we will set up our banners! May the Lord fulfill all your petitions.

Ps. 21:1 - The king shall have joy in Your strength, O Lord; And in Your salvation how greatly shall he rejoice!

Ps. 30:1 - I will extol You, O Lord, for You have lifted me up, And have not let my foes rejoice over me.

Ps. 31:7 - I will be glad and rejoice in Your mercy, For You have considered my trouble; You have known my soul in adversities.

Ps. 32:11 - Be glad in the Lord and rejoice, you righteous; And shout for joy, all you upright in heart!

Ps. 33:1 - Rejoice in the Lord, O you righteous! For praise from the upright is beautiful.

Ps. 33:21 - For our heart shall rejoice in Him, Because we have trusted in His holy name.

Ps. 35:9 - And my soul shall be joyful in the Lord; It shall rejoice in His salvation.

Ps. 35:19 - Let them not rejoice over me who are wrongfully my enemies; Nor let them wink with the eye who hate me without a cause.

Ps. 35:24 - Vindicate me, O Lord my God, according to Your righteousness; And let them not rejoice over me.

Ps. 35:26 - Let them be ashamed and brought to mutual confusion Who rejoice at my hurt; Let them be clothed with shame and dishonor Who exalt themselves against me.

Ps. 38:16 - For I said, "Hear me, lest they rejoice over me, Lest, when my foot slips, they exalt themselves against me."

Ps. 40:16 - Let all those who seek You rejoice and be glad in You; Let such as love Your salvation say continually, "The Lord be magnified!"

Ps. 48:11 - Let Mount Zion rejoice, Let the daughters of Judah be glad, Because of Your judgments.

Ps. 51:8 - Make me hear joy and gladness, That the bones You have broken may rejoice.

Ps. 53:6 - Oh, that the salvation of Israel would come out of Zion! When God brings back the captivity of His people, Let Jacob rejoice and Israel be glad.

Ps. 58:10 - The righteous shall rejoice when he sees the vengeance; He shall wash his feet in the blood of the wicked.

Ps. 60:6 - God has spoken in His holiness: "I will rejoice; I will divide Shechem And measure out the Valley of Succoth.

Ps. 63:7 - Because You have been my help, Therefore in the shadow of Your wings I will rejoice.

Ps. 63:11 - But the king shall rejoice in God; Everyone who swears by Him shall glory; But the mouth of those who speak lies shall be stopped.

Ps. 65:8 - They also who dwell in the farthest parts are afraid of Your signs; You make the outgoings of the morning and evening rejoice.

Ps. 65:12 - They drop on the pastures of the wilderness, And the little hills rejoice on every side.

Ps. 66:6 - He turned the sea into dry land; They went through the river on foot. There we will rejoice in Him.

Ps. 68:3 - But let the righteous be glad; Let them rejoice before God; Yes, let them rejoice exceedingly.

Ps. 68:4 - Sing to God, sing praises to His name; Extol Him who rides on the clouds, By His name YAH, And rejoice before Him.

Ps. 70:4 - Let all those who seek You rejoice and be glad in You; And let those who love Your salvation say continually, "Let God be magnified!"

Ps. 71:23 - My lips shall greatly rejoice when I sing to You, And my soul, which You have redeemed.

Ps. 85:6 - Will You not revive us again, That Your people may rejoice in You?

Ps. 86:4 - Rejoice the soul of Your servant, For to You, O Lord, I lift up my soul.

Ps. 89:12 - The north and the south, You have created them; Tabor and Hermon rejoice in Your name.

Ps. 89:16 - In Your name they rejoice all day long, And in Your righteousness they are exalted.

Ps. 89:42 - You have exalted the right hand of his adversaries; You have made all his enemies rejoice.

Ps. 90:14 - Oh, satisfy us early with Your mercy, That we may rejoice and be glad all our days!

Ps. 96:11 - Let the heavens rejoice, and let the earth be glad; Let the sea roar, and all its fullness.

Ps. 96:12 - Let the field be joyful, and all that is in it. Then all the trees of the woods will rejoice.

Ps. 97:1 - The Lord reigns; Let the earth rejoice; Let the multitude of isles be glad!

Ps. 97:8 - Zion hears and is glad, And the daughters of Judah rejoice Because of Your judgments, O Lord.

Ps. 97:12 - Rejoice in the Lord, you righteous, And give thanks at the remembrance of His holy name.

Ps. 98:4 - Shout joyfully to the Lord, all the earth; Break forth in song, rejoice, and sing praises.

Ps. 104:31 - May the glory of the Lord endure forever; May the Lord rejoice in His works.

Ps. 105:3 - Glory in His holy name; Let the hearts of those rejoice who seek the Lord!

Ps. 106:5 - That I may see the benefit of Your chosen ones, That I may rejoice in the gladness of Your nation, That I may glory with Your inheritance.

Ps. 107:42 - The righteous see it and rejoice, And all iniquity stops its mouth.

Ps. 108:7 - God has spoken in His holiness: "I will rejoice; I will divide Shechem And measure out the Valley of Succoth."

Ps. 109:28 - Let them curse, but You bless; When they arise, let them be ashamed, But let Your servant rejoice.

Ps. 118:24 - This is the day the Lord has made; We will rejoice and be glad in it.

Ps. 119:162 - I rejoice at Your word As one who finds great treasure.

Ps. 149:2 - Let Israel rejoice in their Maker; Let the children of Zion be joyful in their King.

RESCUE

Ps. 22:8 - He trusted in the Lord, let Him rescue Him; Let Him deliver Him, since He delights in Him!

Ps. 35:17 - Lord, how long will You look on? Rescue me from their destructions, My precious life from the lions.

Ps. 144:7 - Stretch out Your hand from above; Rescue me and deliver me out of great waters, From the hand of foreigners.

Ps. 144:11 - Rescue me and deliver me from the hand of foreigners, Whose mouth speaks lying words, And whose right hand is a right hand of falsehood.

REVERENCE

Ps. 89:7 - God is greatly to be feared in the assembly of the saints, And to be held in reverence by all those around Him.

ROCK

Ps. 18:2 - The Lord is my rock and my fortress and my deliverer; My God, my strength, in whom I will trust; My shield and the horn of my salvation, my stronghold.

Ps. 18:31 - For who is God, except the Lord? And who is a rock, except our God?

Ps. 18:46 - The Lord lives! Blessed be my Rock! Let the God of my salvation be exalted.

Ps. 27:5 - For in the time of trouble He shall hide me in His pavilion; In the secret place of His tabernacle He shall hide me; He shall set me high upon a rock.

Ps. 28:1 - To You I will cry, O Lord my Rock: Do not be silent to me, Lest, if You are silent to me, I become like those who go down to the pit.

Ps. 31:2 - Bow down Your ear to me, Deliver me speedily; Be my rock of refuge, A fortress of defense to save me.

Ps. 31:3 - For You are my rock and my fortress; Therefore, for Your name's sake, Lead me and guide me.

Ps. 40:2 - He also brought me up out of a horrible pit, Out of the miry clay, And set my feet upon a rock, And established my steps.

Ps. 42:9 - I will say to God my Rock, "Why have You forgotten me? Why do I go mourning because of the oppression of the enemy?"

Ps. 61:2 - From the end of the earth I will cry to You, When my heart is overwhelmed; Lead me to the rock that is higher than I.

Ps. 62:2 - He only is my rock and my salvation; He is my defense; I shall not be greatly moved.

Ps. 62:6 - He only is my rock and my salvation; He is my defense; I shall not be moved.

Ps. 62:7 - In God is my salvation and my glory; The rock of my strength, And my refuge, is in God.

Ps. 71:3 - Be my strong refuge, To which I may resort continually; You have given the commandment to save me, For You are my rock and my fortress.

Ps. 78:16 - He also brought streams out of the rock, And caused waters to run down like rivers.

Ps. 78:20 - Behold, He struck the rock, So that the waters gushed out, And the streams overflowed. Can He give bread also? Can He provide meat for His people?

Ps. 78:35 - Then they remembered that God was their rock, And the Most High God their Redeemer.

Ps. 81:16 - He would have fed them also with the finest of wheat; And with honey from the rock I would have satisfied you.

Ps. 89:26 - He shall cry to Me, "You are my Father, My God, and the rock of my salvation."

Ps. 92:15 - To declare that the Lord is upright; He is my rock, and there is no unrighteousness in Him.

Ps. 94:22 - But the Lord has been my defense, And my God the rock of my refuge.

Ps. 95:1 - Oh come, let us sing to the Lord! Let us shout joyfully to the Rock of our salvation.

Ps. 104:18 - The high hills are for the wild goats; The cliffs are a refuge for the rock badgers.

Ps. 105:41 - He opened the rock, and water gushed out; It ran in the dry places like a river.

Ps. 114:8 - Who turned the rock into a pool of water, The flint into a fountain of waters.

Ps. 137:9 - Happy the one who takes and dashes Your little ones against the rock!

Ps. 144:1 - Blessed be the Lord my Rock, Who trains my hands for war, And my fingers for battle.

SALVATION

Ps. 3:8 - Salvation belongs to the Lord. Your blessing is upon Your people.

Ps. 9:14 - That I may tell of all Your praise In the gates of the daughter of Zion. I will rejoice in Your salvation.

Ps. 13:5 - But I have trusted in Your mercy; My heart shall rejoice in Your salvation.

Ps. 14:7 - Oh, that the salvation of Israel would come out of Zion! When the Lord brings back the captivity of His people, Let Jacob rejoice and Israel be glad.

Ps. 18:2 - The Lord is my rock and my fortress and my deliverer; My God, my strength, in whom I will trust; My shield and the horn of my salvation, my stronghold.

Ps. 18:35 - You have also given me the shield of Your salvation; Your right hand has held me up, Your gentleness has made me great.

Ps. 18:46 - The Lord lives! Blessed be my Rock! Let the God of my salvation be exalted.

Ps. 20:5 - We will rejoice in your salvation, And in the name of our God we will set up our banners! May the Lord fulfill all your petitions.

Ps. 21:1 - The king shall have joy in Your strength, O Lord; And in Your salvation how greatly shall he rejoice!

Ps. 21:5 - His glory is great in Your salvation; Honor and majesty You have placed upon him.

Ps. 24:5 - He shall receive blessing from the Lord, And righteousness from the God of his salvation.

Ps. 25:5 - Lead me in Your truth and teach me, For You are the God of my salvation; On You I wait all the day.

Ps. 27:1 - The Lord is my light and my salvation; Whom shall I fear? The Lord is the strength of my life; Of whom shall I be afraid?

Ps. 27:9 - Do not hide Your face from me; Do not turn Your servant away in anger; You have been my help; Do not leave me nor forsake me, O God of my salvation.

Ps. 35:3 - Also draw out the spear, And stop those who pursue me. Say to my soul, "I am your salvation."

Ps. 35:9 - And my soul shall be joyful in the Lord; It shall rejoice in His salvation.

Ps. 37:39 - But the salvation of the righteous is from the Lord; He is their strength in the time of trouble.

Ps. 38:22 - Make haste to help me, O Lord, my salvation!

Ps. 40:10 - I have not hidden Your righteousness within my heart; I have declared Your faithfulness and Your salvation; I have not concealed Your lovingkindness and Your truth From the great assembly.

Ps. 40:16 - Let all those who seek You rejoice and be glad in You; Let such as love Your salvation say continually, "The Lord be magnified!"

Ps. 50:23 - Whoever offers praise glorifies Me; And to him who orders his conduct aright I will show the salvation of God.

Ps. 51:12 - Restore to me the joy of Your salvation, And uphold me by Your generous Spirit.

Ps. 51:14 - Deliver me from the guilt of bloodshed, O God, The God of my salvation, And my tongue shall sing aloud of Your righteousness.

Ps. 53:6 - Oh, that the salvation of Israel would come out of Zion! When God brings back the captivity of His people, Let Jacob rejoice and Israel be glad.

Ps. 62:1 - Truly my soul silently waits for God; From Him comes my salvation.

Ps. 62:2 - He only is my rock and my salvation; He is my defense; I shall not be greatly moved.

Ps. 62:6 - He only is my rock and my salvation; He is my defense; I shall not be moved.

Ps. 62:7 - In God is my salvation and my glory; The rock of my strength, And my refuge, is in God.

Ps. 65:5 - By awesome deeds in righteousness You will answer us, O God of our salvation, You who are the confidence of all the ends of the earth, And of the far-off seas.

Ps. 67:2 - That Your way may be known on earth, Your salvation among all nations.

Ps. 68:19 - Blessed be the Lord, Who daily loads us with benefits, The God of our salvation!

Ps. 68:20 - Our God is the God of salvation; And to God the Lord belong escapes from death.

Ps. 69:13 - But as for me, my prayer is to You, O Lord, in the acceptable time; O God, in the multitude of Your mercy, Hear me in the truth of Your salvation.

Ps. 69:29 - But I am poor and sorrowful; Let Your salvation, O God, set me up on high.

Ps. 70:4 - Let all those who seek You rejoice and be glad in You; And let those who love Your salvation say continually, "Let God be magnified!"

Ps. 71:15 - My mouth shall tell of Your righteousness And Your salvation all the day, For I do not know their limits.

Ps. 74:12 - For God is my King from of old, Working salvation in the midst of the earth.

Ps. 78:22 - Because they did not believe in God, And did not trust in His salvation.

Ps. 79:9 - Help us, O God of our salvation, For the glory of Your name; And deliver us, and provide atonement for our sins, For Your name's sake!

Ps. 85:4 - Restore us, O God of our salvation, And cause Your anger toward us to cease.

Ps. 85:7 - Show us Your mercy, Lord, And grant us Your salvation.

Ps. 85:9 - Surely His salvation is near to those who fear Him, That glory may dwell in our land.

Ps. 88:1 - O Lord, God of my salvation, I have cried out day and night before You.

Ps. 89:26 - He shall cry to Me, "You are my Father, My God, and the rock of my salvation."

Ps. 91:16 - With long life I will satisfy him, And show him My salvation.

Ps. 95:1 - Oh come, let us sing to the Lord! Let us shout joyfully to the Rock of our salvation.

Ps. 96:2 - Sing to the Lord, bless His name; Proclaim the good news of His salvation from day to day.

Ps. 98:2 - The Lord has made known His salvation; His righteousness He has revealed in the sight of the nations.

Ps. 98:3 - He has remembered His mercy and His faithfulness to the house of Israel; All the ends of the earth have seen the salvation of our God.

Ps. 106:4 - Remember me, O Lord, with the favor You have toward Your people; Oh, visit me with Your salvation

Ps. 116:13 - I will take up the cup of salvation, And call upon the name of the Lord.

Ps. 118:14 - The Lord is my strength and song, And He has become my salvation.

Ps. 118:15 - The voice of rejoicing and salvation Is in the tents of the righteous; The right hand of the Lord does valiantly.

Ps. 118:21 - I will praise You, For You have answered me, And have become my salvation.

Ps. 119:41 - Let Your mercies come also to me, O Lord — Your salvation according to Your word.

Ps. 119:81 - My soul faints for Your salvation, But I hope in Your word.

Ps. 119:123 - My eyes fail from seeking Your salvation And Your righteous word.

Ps. 119:155 - Salvation is far from the wicked, For they do not seek Your statutes.

Ps. 119:166 - Lord, I hope for Your salvation, And I do Your commandments.

Ps. 119:174 - I long for Your salvation, O Lord, And Your law is my delight.

Ps. 132:16 - I will also clothe her priests with salvation, And her saints shall shout aloud for joy.

Ps. 140:7 - O God the Lord, the strength of my salvation, You have covered my head in the day of battle.

Ps. 144:10 - The One who gives salvation to kings, Who delivers David His servant From the deadly sword.

Ps. 149:4 - For the Lord takes pleasure in His people; He will beautify the humble with salvation.

SAVE

Ps. 3:7 - Arise, O Lord; Save me, O my God! For You have struck all my enemies on the cheekbone; You have broken the teeth of the ungodly.

Ps. 6:4 - Return, O Lord, deliver me! Oh, save me for Your mercies' sake!

Ps. 7:1 - O Lord my God, in You I put my trust; Save me from all those who persecute me; And deliver me.

Ps. 17:7 - Show Your marvelous lovingkindness by Your right hand, O You who save those who trust in You From those who rise up against them.

Ps. 18:27 - For You will save the humble people, But will bring down haughty looks.

Ps. 18:41 - They cried out, but there was none to save; Even to the Lord, but He did not answer them.

Ps. 20:9 - Save, Lord! May the King answer us when we call.

Ps. 22:21 - Save Me from the lion's mouth And from the horns of the wild oxen! You have answered Me.

Ps. 28:9 - Save Your people, And bless Your inheritance; Shepherd them also, And bear them up forever.

Ps. 31:2 - Bow down Your ear to me, Deliver me speedily; Be my rock of refuge, A fortress of defense to save me.

Ps. 31:16 - Make Your face shine upon Your servant; Save me for Your mercies' sake.

Ps. 37:40 - And the Lord shall help them and deliver them; He shall deliver them from the wicked, And save them, Because they trust in Him.

Ps. 44:3 - For they did not gain possession of the land by their own sword, Nor did their own arm save them; But it was Your right hand, Your arm, and the light of Your countenance, Because You favored them.

Ps. 44:6 - For I will not trust in my bow, Nor shall my sword save me.

Ps. 54:1 - Save me, O God, by Your name, And vindicate me by Your strength.

Ps. 55:16 - As for me, I will call upon God, And the Lord shall save me.

Ps. 57:3 - He shall send from heaven and save me; He reproaches the one who would swallow me up. Selah God shall send forth His mercy and His truth.

Ps. 59:2 - Deliver me from the workers of iniquity, And save me from bloodthirsty men.

Ps. 60:5 - That Your beloved may be delivered, Save with Your right hand, and hear me.

Ps. 69:1 - Save me, O God! For the waters have come up to my neck.

Ps. 69:35 - For God will save Zion And build the cities of Judah, That they may dwell there and possess it.

Ps. 71:2 - Deliver me in Your righteousness, and cause me to escape; Incline Your ear to me, and save me.

Ps. 71:3 - Be my strong refuge, To which I may resort continually; You have given the commandment to save me, For You are my rock and my fortress.

Ps. 72:4 - He will bring justice to the poor of the people; He will save the children of the needy, And will break in pieces the oppressor.

Ps. 72:13 - He will spare the poor and needy, And will save the souls of the needy.

Ps. 80:2 - Before Ephraim, Benjamin, and Manasseh, Stir up Your strength, And come and save us!

Ps. 86:2 - Preserve my life, for I am holy; You are my God; Save Your servant who trusts in You!

Ps. 86:16 - Oh, turn to me, and have mercy on me! Give Your strength to Your servant, And save the son of Your maidservant.

Ps. 106:47 - Save us, O Lord our God, And gather us from among the Gentiles, To give thanks to Your holy name, To triumph in Your praise.

Ps. 108:6 - That Your beloved may be delivered, Save with Your right hand, and hear me.

Ps. 109:26 - Help me, O Lord my God! Oh, save me according to Your mercy.

Ps. 109:31 - For He shall stand at the right hand of the poor, To save him from those who condemn him.

Ps. 118:25 - Save now, I pray, O Lord; O Lord, I pray, send now prosperity.

Ps. 119:94 - I am Yours, save me; For I have sought Your precepts.

Ps. 119:146 - I cry out to You; Save me, and I will keep Your testimonies.

Ps. 138:7 - Though I walk in the midst of trouble, You will revive me; You will stretch out Your hand Against the wrath of my enemies, And Your right hand will save me.

Ps. 145:19 - He will fulfill the desire of those who fear Him; He also will hear their cry and save them.

SEED

Ps. 89:4 - Your seed I will establish forever, And build up your throne to all generations.

Ps. 89:29 - His seed also I will make to endure forever, And his throne as the days of heaven.

Ps. 89:36 - His seed shall endure forever, And his throne as the sun before Me.

Ps. 105:6 - O seed of Abraham His servant, You children of Jacob, His chosen ones!

Ps. 126:6 - He who continually goes forth weeping, Bearing seed for sowing, Shall doubtless come again with rejoicing, Bringing his sheaves with him.

SHADOW

Ps. 17:8 - Keep me as the apple of Your eye; Hide me under the shadow of Your wings.

Ps. 23:4 - Yea, though I walk through the valley of the shadow of death, I will fear no evil; For You are with me; Your rod and Your staff, they comfort me.

Ps. 36:7 - How precious is Your lovingkindness, O God! Therefore the children of men put their trust under the shadow of Your wings.

Ps. 39:6 - Surely every man walks about like a shadow; Surely they busy themselves in vain; He heaps up riches, And does not know who will gather them.

Ps. 44:19 - But You have severely broken us in the place of jackals, And covered us with the shadow of death.

Ps. 57:1 - Be merciful to me, O God, be merciful to me! For my soul trusts in You; And in the shadow of Your wings I will make my refuge, Until these calamities have passed by.

Ps. 63:7 - Because You have been my help, Therefore in the shadow of Your wings I will rejoice.

Ps. 80:10 - The hills were covered with its shadow, And the mighty cedars with its boughs.

Ps. 91:1 - He who dwells in the secret place of the Most High Shall abide under the shadow of the Almighty.

Ps. 102:11 - My days are like a shadow that lengthens, And I wither away like grass.

Ps. 107:10 - Those who sat in darkness and in the shadow of death, Bound in affliction and irons.

Ps. 107:14 - He brought them out of darkness and the shadow of death, And broke their chains in pieces.

Ps. 109:23 - I am gone like a shadow when it lengthens; I am shaken off like a locust.

Ps. 144:4 - Man is like a breath; His days are like a passing shadow.

SHEILD

Ps. 3:3 - But You, O Lord, are a shield for me, My glory and the One who lifts up my head.

Ps. 5:12 - For You, O Lord, will bless the righteous; With favor You will surround him as with a shield.

Ps. 18:2 - The Lord is my rock and my fortress and my deliverer; My God, my strength, in whom I will trust; My shield and the horn of my salvation, my stronghold.

Chapter Two

Ps. 18:30 - As for God, His way is perfect; The word of the Lord is proven; He is a shield to all who trust in Him.

Ps. 18:35 - You have also given me the shield of Your salvation; Your right hand has held me up, Your gentleness has made me great.

Ps. 28:7 - The Lord is my strength and my shield; My heart trusted in Him, and I am helped; Therefore my heart greatly rejoices, And with my song I will praise Him.

Ps. 33:20 - Our soul waits for the Lord; He is our help and our shield.

Ps. 35:2 - Take hold of shield and buckler, And stand up for my help.

Ps. 59:11 - Do not slay them, lest my people forget; Scatter them by Your power, And bring them down, O Lord our shield.

Ps. 76:3 - There He broke the arrows of the bow, The shield and sword of battle.

Ps. 84:9 - O God, behold our shield, And look upon the face of Your anointed.

Ps. 84:11 - For the Lord God is a sun and shield; The Lord will give grace and glory; No good thing will He withhold From those who walk uprightly.

Ps. 89:18 - For our shield belongs to the Lord, And our king to the Holy One of Israel.

Ps. 91:4 - He shall cover you with His feathers, And under His wings you shall take refuge; His truth shall be your shield and buckler.

Ps. 115:9 - O Israel, trust in the Lord; He is their help and their shield.

Ps. 115:10 - O house of Aaron, trust in the Lord; He is their help and their shield.

Ps. 115:11 - You who fear the Lord, trust in the Lord; He is their help and their shield.

Ps. 119:114 - You are my hiding place and my shield; I hope in Your word.

Ps. 144:2 - My lovingkindness and my fortress, My high tower and my deliverer, My shield and the One in whom I take refuge, Who subdues my people under me.

SHELTER

Ps. 61:3 - For You have been a shelter for me, A strong tower from the enemy.

Ps. 61:4 - I will abide in Your tabernacle forever; I will trust in the shelter of Your wings.

Ps. 143:9 - Deliver me, O Lord, from my enemies; In You I take shelter.

SILVER

Ps. 12:6 - The words of the Lord are pure words, Like silver tried in a furnace of earth, Purified seven times.

Ps. 66:10 - For You, O God, have tested us; You have refined us as silver is refined.

Ps. 68:13 - Though you lie down among the sheepfolds, You will be like the wings of a dove covered with silver, And her feathers with yellow gold.

Ps. 68:30 - Rebuke the beasts of the reeds, The herd of bulls with the calves of the peoples, Till everyone submits himself with pieces of silver. Scatter the peoples who delight in war.

Ps. 105:37 - He also brought them out with silver and gold, And there was none feeble among His tribes.

Ps. 115:4 - Their idols are silver and gold, The work of men's hands.

Ps. 119:72 - The law of Your mouth is better to me Than thousands of coins of gold and silver.

Ps. 135:15 - The idols of the nations are silver and gold, The work of men's hands.

SPLENDOR

Ps. 37:20 - But the wicked shall perish; And the enemies of the Lord, Like the splendor of the meadows, shall vanish. Into smoke they shall vanish away.

Ps. 145:5 - I will meditate on the glorious splendor of Your majesty, And on Your wondrous works.

STRAIGHT

Ps. 5:8 - Lead me, O Lord, in Your righteousness because of my enemies; Make Your way straight before my face.

SUPPLICATION

Ps. 6:9 - The Lord has heard my supplication; The Lord will receive my prayer.

Ps. 30:8 - I cried out to You, O Lord; And to the Lord I made supplication.

Ps. 55:1 - Give ear to my prayer, O God, And do not hide Yourself from my supplication.

Ps. 119:170 - Let my supplication come before You; Deliver me according to Your word.

Ps. 142:1 - I cry out to the Lord with my voice; With my voice to the Lord I make my supplication.

SWEET

Ps. 55:14 - We took sweet counsel together, And walked to the house of God in the throng.

Ps. 66:15 - I will offer You burnt sacrifices of fat animals, With the sweet aroma of rams; I will offer bulls with goats.

Ps. 104:34 - May my meditation be sweet to Him; I will be glad in the Lord.

Ps. 119:103 - How sweet are Your words to my taste, Sweeter than honey to my mouth!

Ps. 141:6 - Their judges are overthrown by the sides of the cliff, And they hear my words, for they are sweet.

TEMPLE

Ps. 5:7 - But as for me, I will come into Your house in the multitude of Your mercy; In fear of You I will worship toward Your holy temple.

Ps. 11:4 - The Lord is in His holy temple, The Lord's throne is in heaven; His eyes behold, His eyelids test the sons of men.

Ps. 18:6 - In my distress I called upon the Lord, And cried out to my God; He heard my voice from His temple, And my cry came before Him, even to His ears.

Ps. 27:4 - One thing I have desired of the Lord, That will I seek: That I may dwell in the house of the Lord All the days of my life, To behold the beauty of the Lord, And to inquire in His temple.

Ps. 29:9 - The voice of the Lord makes the deer give birth, And strips the forests bare; And in His temple everyone says, "Glory!"

Ps. 48:9 - We have thought, O God, on Your lovingkindness, In the midst of Your temple.

Ps. 65:4 - Blessed is the man You choose, And cause to approach You, That he may dwell in Your courts. We shall be satisfied with the goodness of Your house, Of Your holy temple.

Ps. 68:29 - Because of Your temple at Jerusalem, Kings will bring presents to You.

Ps. 79:1 - O God, the nations have come into Your inheritance; Your holy temple they have defiled; They have laid Jerusalem in heaps.

Ps. 138:2 - I will worship toward Your holy temple, And praise Your name For Your lovingkindness and

Your truth; For You have magnified Your word above all Your name.

THRONE

Ps. 9:4 - For You have maintained my right and my cause; You sat on the throne judging in righteousness.

Ps. 9:7 - But the Lord shall endure forever; He has prepared His throne for judgment.

Ps. 11:4 - The Lord is in His holy temple, The Lord's throne is in heaven; His eyes behold, His eyelids test the sons of men.

Ps. 45:6 - Your throne, O God, is forever and ever; A scepter of righteousness is the scepter of Your kingdom.

Ps. 47:8 - God reigns over the nations; God sits on His holy throne.

Ps. 89:4 - Your seed I will establish forever, And build up your throne to all generations.

Ps. 89:14 - Righteousness and justice are the foundation of Your throne; Mercy and truth go before Your face.

Ps. 89:29 - His seed also I will make to endure forever, And his throne as the days of heaven.

Ps. 89:36 - His seed shall endure forever, And his throne as the sun before Me.

Ps. 89:44 - You have made his glory cease, And cast his throne down to the ground.

Ps. 93:2 - Your throne is established from of old; You are from everlasting.

Ps. 94:20 - Shall the throne of iniquity, which devises evil by law, Have fellowship with You?

Ps. 97:2 - Clouds and darkness surround Him; Righteousness and justice are the foundation of His throne.

Ps. 103:19 - The Lord has established His throne in heaven, And His kingdom rules over all.

Ps. 132:11 - The Lord has sworn in truth to David; He will not turn from it: "I will set upon your throne the fruit of your body."

Ps. 132:12 - If your sons will keep My covenant And My testimony which I shall teach them, Their sons also shall sit upon your throne forevermore.

TRUST

Ps. 2:12 - Kiss the Son, lest He be angry, And you perish in the way, When His wrath is kindled but a little. Blessed are all those who put their trust in Him.

Ps. 4:5 - Offer the sacrifices of righteousness, And put your trust in the Lord.

Ps. 5:11 - But let all those rejoice who put their trust in You; Let them ever shout for joy, because You defend them; Let those also who love Your name Be joyful in You.

Ps. 7:1 - O Lord my God, in You I put my trust; Save me from all those who persecute me; And deliver me.

Ps. 9:10 - And those who know Your name will put their trust in You; For You, Lord, have not forsaken those who seek You.

Ps. 11:1 - In the Lord I put my trust; How can you say to my soul, "Flee as a bird to your mountain"?

Ps. 16:1 - Preserve me, O God, for in You I put my trust.

Ps. 17:7 - Show Your marvelous lovingkindness by Your right hand, O You who save those who trust in You From those who rise up against them.

Ps. 18:2 - The Lord is my rock and my fortress and my deliverer; My God, my strength, in whom I will trust; My shield and the horn of my salvation, my stronghold.

Ps. 18:30 - As for God, His way is perfect; The word of the Lord is proven; He is a shield to all who trust in Him.

Ps. 20:7 - Some trust in chariots, and some in horses; But we will remember the name of the Lord our God.

Ps. 22:9 - But You are He who took Me out of the womb; You made Me trust while on My mother's breasts.

Ps. 25:2 - O my God, I trust in You; Let me not be ashamed; Let not my enemies triumph over me.

Ps. 25:20 - Keep my soul, and deliver me; Let me not be ashamed, for I put my trust in You.

Ps. 31:1 - In You, O Lord, I put my trust; Let me never be ashamed; Deliver me in Your righteousness.

Ps. 31:6 - I have hated those who regard useless idols; But I trust in the Lord.

Ps. 31:14 - But as for me, I trust in You, O Lord; I say, "You are my God."

Ps. 31:19 - Oh, how great is Your goodness, Which You have laid up for those who fear You, Which You have prepared for those who trust in You In the presence of the sons of men!

Ps. 34:22 - The Lord redeems the soul of His servants, And none of those who trust in Him shall be condemned.

Ps. 36:7 - How precious is Your lovingkindness, O God! Therefore the children of men put their trust under the shadow of Your wings.

Ps. 37:3 - Trust in the Lord, and do good; Dwell in the land, and feed on His faithfulness.

Ps. 37:5 - Commit your way to the Lord, Trust also in Him, And He shall bring it to pass.

Ps. 37:40 - And the Lord shall help them and deliver them; He shall deliver them from the wicked, And save them, Because they trust in Him.

Ps. 40:3 - He has put a new song in my mouth—Praise to our God; Many will see it and fear, And will trust in the Lord.

Ps. 40:4 - Blessed is that man who makes the Lord his trust, And does not respect the proud, nor such as turn aside to lies.

Ps. 44:6 - For I will not trust in my bow, Nor shall my sword save me.

Ps. 49:6 - Those who trust in their wealth And boast in the multitude of their riches.

Ps. 52:8 - But I am like a green olive tree in the house of God; I trust in the mercy of God forever and ever.

Ps. 55:23 - But You, O God, shall bring them down to the pit of destruction; Bloodthirsty and deceitful men shall not live out half their days; But I will trust in You.

Ps. 56:3 - Whenever I am afraid, I will trust in You.

Ps. 56:4 - In God (I will praise His word), In God I have put my trust; I will not fear. What can flesh do to me?

Ps. 56:11 - In God I have put my trust; I will not be afraid. What can man do to me?

Ps. 61:4 - I will abide in Your tabernacle forever; I will trust in the shelter of Your wings.

Ps. 62:8 - Trust in Him at all times, you people; Pour out your heart before Him; God is a refuge for us.

Ps. 62:10 - Do not trust in oppression, Nor vainly hope in robbery; If riches increase, Do not set your heart on them.

Ps. 64:10 - The righteous shall be glad in the Lord, and trust in Him. And all the upright in heart shall glory.

Ps. 71:1 - In You, O Lord, I put my trust; Let me never be put to shame.

Ps. 71:5 - For You are my hope, O Lord God; You are my trust from my youth.

Ps. 73:28 - But it is good for me to draw near to God; I have put my trust in the Lord God, That I may declare all Your works.

Ps. 78:22 - Because they did not believe in God, And did not trust in His salvation.

Ps. 91:2 - I will say of the Lord, "He is my refuge and my fortress; My God, in Him I will trust."

Ps. 115:9 - O Israel, trust in the Lord; He is their help and their shield.

Ps. 115:10 - O house of Aaron, trust in the Lord; He is their help and their shield.

Ps. 115:11 - You who fear the Lord, trust in the Lord; He is their help and their shield.

Ps. 118:8 - It is better to trust in the Lord Than to put confidence in man.

Ps. 118:9 - It is better to trust in the Lord Than to put confidence in princes.

Ps. 119:42 - So shall I have an answer for him who reproaches me, For I trust in Your word.

Ps. 125:1 - Those who trust in the Lord Are like Mount Zion, Which cannot be moved, but abides forever.

Ps. 143:8 - Cause me to hear Your lovingkindness in the morning, For in You do I trust; Cause me to know the way in which I should walk, For I lift up my soul to You.

Ps. 146:3 - Do not put your trust in princes, Nor in a son of man, in whom there is no help.

UNDERSTANDING

Ps. 32:9 - Do not be like the horse or like the mule, Which have no understanding, Which must be harnessed with bit and bridle, Else they will not come near you.

Ps. 47:7 - For God is the King of all the earth; Sing praises with understanding.

Ps. 49:3 - My mouth shall speak wisdom, And the meditation of my heart shall give understanding.

Ps. 111:10 - The fear of the Lord is the beginning of wisdom; A good understanding have all those who do His commandments. His praise endures forever.

Ps. 119:34 - Give me understanding, and I shall keep Your law; Indeed, I shall observe it with my whole heart.

Ps. 119:73 - Your hands have made me and fashioned me; Give me understanding, that I may learn Your commandments.

Ps. 119:99 - I have more understanding than all my teachers, For Your testimonies are my meditation.

Ps. 119:104 - Through Your precepts I get understanding; Therefore I hate every false way.

Ps. 119:125 - I am Your servant; Give me understanding, That I may know Your testimonies.

Ps. 119:130 - The entrance of Your words gives light; It gives understanding to the simple.

Ps. 119:144 - The righteousness of Your testimonies is everlasting; Give me understanding, and I shall live.

Ps. 119:169 - Let my cry come before You, O Lord; Give me understanding according to Your word.

Ps. 147:5 - Great is our Lord, and mighty in power; His understanding is infinite.

UPHOLDS

Ps. 37:17 - For the arms of the wicked shall be broken, But the Lord upholds the righteous.

Ps. 37:24 - Though he fall, he shall not be utterly cast down; For the Lord upholds him with His hand.

Ps. 63:8 - My soul follows close behind You; Your right hand upholds me.

Ps. 145:14 - The Lord upholds all who fall, And raises up all who are bowed down.

UPRIGHT

Ps. 7:10 - My defense is of God, Who saves the upright in heart.

Ps. 11:2 - For look! The wicked bend their bow, They make ready their arrow on the string, That they may shoot secretly at the upright in heart.

Ps. 11:7 - For the Lord is righteous, He loves righteousness; His countenance beholds the upright.

Ps. 17:2 - Let my vindication come from Your presence; Let Your eyes look on the things that are upright.

Ps. 20:8 - They have bowed down and fallen; But we have risen and stand upright.

Ps. 25:8 - Good and upright is the Lord; Therefore He teaches sinners in the way.

Ps. 32:11 - Be glad in the Lord and rejoice, you righteous; And shout for joy, all you upright in heart!

Ps. 33:1 - Rejoice in the Lord, O you righteous! For praise from the upright is beautiful.

Ps. 36:10 - Oh, continue Your lovingkindness to those who know You, And Your righteousness to the upright in heart.

Ps. 37:14 - The wicked have drawn the sword And have bent their bow, To cast down the poor and needy, To slay those who are of upright conduct.

Ps. 37:18 - The Lord knows the days of the upright, And their inheritance shall be forever.

Ps. 37:37 - Mark the blameless man, and observe the upright; For the future of that man is peace.

Ps. 49:14 - Like sheep they are laid in the grave; Death shall feed on them; The upright shall have dominion over them in the morning; And their beauty shall be consumed in the grave, far from their dwelling.

Ps. 64:10 - The righteous shall be glad in the Lord, and trust in Him. And all the upright in heart shall glory.

Ps. 92:15 - To declare that the Lord is upright; He is my rock, and there is no unrighteousness in Him.

Ps. 94:15 - But judgment will return to righteousness, And all the upright in heart will follow it.

Ps. 97:11 - Light is sown for the righteous, And gladness for the upright in heart.

Ps. 111:1 - Praise the Lord! I will praise the Lord with my whole heart, In the assembly of the upright and in the congregation.

Ps. 112:2 - His descendants will be mighty on earth; The generation of the upright will be blessed.

Ps. 112:4 - Unto the upright there arises light in the darkness; He is gracious, and full of compassion, and righteous.

Ps. 119:137 - Righteous are You, O Lord, And upright are Your judgments.

Ps. 125:4 - Do good, O Lord, to those who are good, And to those who are upright in their hearts.

Ps. 140:13 - Surely the righteous shall give thanks to Your name; The upright shall dwell in Your presence.

VICTORY

Ps. 98:1 - Oh, sing to the Lord a new song! For He has done marvelous things; His right hand and His holy arm have gained Him the victory.

VINDICATE

Ps. 26:1 - Vindicate me, O Lord, For I have walked in my integrity. I have also trusted in the Lord; I shall not slip.

Ps. 35:24 - Vindicate me, O Lord my God, according to Your righteousness; And let them not rejoice over me.

Ps. 43:1 - Vindicate me, O God, And plead my cause against an ungodly nation; Oh, deliver me from the deceitful and unjust man!

Ps. 54:1 - Save me, O God, by Your name, And vindicate me by Your strength.

WANT
Ps. 23:1 - The Lord is my shepherd; I shall not want.
Ps. 34:9 - Oh, fear the Lord, you His saints! There is no want to those who fear Him.

WISDOM
Ps. 37:30 - The mouth of the righteous speaks wisdom, And his tongue talks of justice.
Ps. 49:3 - My mouth shall speak wisdom, And the meditation of my heart shall give understanding.
Ps. 51:6 - Behold, You desire truth in the inward parts, And in the hidden part You will make me to know wisdom.
Ps. 90:12 - So teach us to number our days, That we may gain a heart of wisdom.
Ps. 104:24 - O Lord, how manifold are Your works! In wisdom You have made them all. The earth is full of Your possessions.
Ps. 105:22 - To bind his princes at his pleasure, And teach his elders wisdom.
Ps. 111:10 - The fear of the Lord is the beginning of wisdom; A good understanding have all those who do His commandments. His praise endures forever.
Ps. 136:5 - To Him who by wisdom made the heavens, For His mercy endures forever.

WISE
Ps. 2:10 - Now therefore, be wise, O kings; Be instructed, you judges of the earth.
Ps. 19:7 - The law of the Lord is perfect, converting the soul; The testimony of the Lord is sure, making wise the simple.

Ps. 36:3 - The words of his mouth are wickedness and deceit; He has ceased to be wise and to do good.

Ps. 49:10 - For he sees wise men die; Likewise the fool and the senseless person perish, And leave their wealth to others.

Ps. 94:8 - Understand, you senseless among the people; And you fools, when will you be wise?

Ps. 107:43 - Whoever is wise will observe these things, And they will understand the lovingkindness of the Lord.

WONDERFUL

Ps. 40:5 - Many, O Lord my God, are Your wonderful works Which You have done; And Your thoughts toward us Cannot be recounted to You in order; If I would declare and speak of them, They are more than can be numbered.

Ps. 78:4 - We will not hide them from their children, Telling to the generation to come the praises of the Lord, And His strength and His wonderful works that He has done.

Ps. 107:8 - Oh, that men would give thanks to the Lord for His goodness, And for His wonderful works to the children of men!

Ps. 107:15 - Oh, that men would give thanks to the Lord for His goodness, And for His wonderful works to the children of men!

Ps. 107:21 - Oh, that men would give thanks to the Lord for His goodness, And for His wonderful works to the children of men!

Ps. 107:31 - Oh, that men would give thanks to the Lord for His goodness, And for His wonderful works to the children of men!

Ps. 111:4 - He has made His wonderful works to be remembered; The Lord is gracious and full of compassion.

Ps. 119:129 - Your testimonies are wonderful; Therefore my soul keeps them.

Ps. 139:6 - Such knowledge is too wonderful for me; It is high, I cannot attain it.

ZION

Ps. 2:6 - Yet I have set My King On My holy hill of Zion.

Ps. 9:11 - Sing praises to the Lord, who dwells in Zion! Declare His deeds among the people.

Ps. 9:14 - That I may tell of all Your praise In the gates of the daughter of Zion. I will rejoice in Your salvation.

Ps. 14:7 - Oh, that the salvation of Israel would come out of Zion! When the Lord brings back the captivity of His people, Let Jacob rejoice and Israel be glad.

Ps. 20:2 - May He send you help from the sanctuary, And strengthen you out of Zion.

Ps. 48:2 - Beautiful in elevation, The joy of the whole earth, Is Mount Zion on the sides of the north, The city of the great King.

Ps. 48:11 - Let Mount Zion rejoice, Let the daughters of Judah be glad, Because of Your judgments.

Ps. 48:12 - Walk about Zion, And go all around her. Count her towers.

Ps. 50:2 - Out of Zion, the perfection of beauty, God will shine forth.

Ps. 51:18 - Do good in Your good pleasure to Zion; Build the walls of Jerusalem.

Ps. 53:6 - Oh, that the salvation of Israel would come out of Zion! When God brings back the captivity of His people, Let Jacob rejoice and Israel be glad.

Ps. 65:1 - Praise is awaiting You, O God, in Zion; And to You the vow shall be performed.

Ps. 69:35 - For God will save Zion And build the cities of Judah, That they may dwell there and possess it.

Ps. 74:2 - Remember Your congregation, which You have purchased of old, The tribe of Your inheritance, which You have redeemed — This Mount Zion where You have dwelt.

Ps. 76:2 - In Salem also is His tabernacle, And His dwelling place in Zion.

Ps. 78:68 - But chose the tribe of Judah, Mount Zion which He loved.

Ps. 84:7 - They go from strength to strength; Each one appears before God in Zion.

Ps. 87:2 - The Lord loves the gates of Zion More than all the dwellings of Jacob.

Ps. 87:5 - And of Zion it will be said, "This one and that one were born in her; And the Most High Himself shall establish her."

Ps. 97:8 - Zion hears and is glad, And the daughters of Judah rejoice Because of Your judgments, O Lord.

Ps. 99:2 - The Lord is great in Zion, And He is high above all the peoples.

Ps. 102:13 - You will arise and have mercy on Zion; For the time to favor her, Yes, the set time, has come.

Ps. 102:16 - For the Lord shall build up Zion; He shall appear in His glory.

Ps. 102:21 - To declare the name of the Lord in Zion, And His praise in Jerusalem.

Ps. 110:2 - The Lord shall send the rod of Your strength out of Zion. Rule in the midst of Your enemies!

Ps. 125:1 - Those who trust in the Lord Are like Mount Zion, Which cannot be moved, but abides forever.

Ps. 126:1 - When the Lord brought back the captivity of Zion, We were like those who dream.

Ps. 128:5 - The Lord bless you out of Zion, And may you see the good of Jerusalem All the days of your life.

Ps. 129:5 - Let all those who hate Zion Be put to shame and turned back.

Ps. 132:13 - For the Lord has chosen Zion; He has desired it for His dwelling place.

Ps. 133:3 - It is like the dew of Hermon, Descending upon the mountains of Zion; For there the Lord commanded the blessing — Life forevermore.

Ps. 134:3 - The Lord who made heaven and earth Bless you from Zion!

Ps. 135:21 - Blessed be the Lord out of Zion, Who dwells in Jerusalem! Praise the Lord!

Ps. 137:1 - By the rivers of Babylon, There we sat down, yea, we wept When we remembered Zion.

Ps. 137:3 - For there those who carried us away captive asked of us a song, And those who plundered us requested mirth, Saying, "Sing us one of the songs of Zion!"

Ps. 146:10 - The Lord shall reign forever — Your God, O Zion, to all generations. Praise the Lord!

Ps. 147:12 - Praise the Lord, O Jerusalem! Praise your God, O Zion!

Ps. 149:2 - Let Israel rejoice in their Maker; Let the children of Zion be joyful in their King.

TOPIC INDEX

MY OTHER PUBLICATIONS

To inquire about other books written by Eugene Carvalho, please visit the website below.

WWW.NEWWINEMISSIONS.INFO

NOTES

NOTES

<u>NOTES</u>